THE LAST STEAM
LOCOMOTIVES OF
WESTERN EUROPE

P. RANSOME-WALLIS

LONDON
IAN ALLAN LTD

CONTENTS

With the exception of Plates 176, 177, 291 and 292, all the photographs reproduced in this book have been taken by the author.

THE LAST STEAM
LOCOMOTIVES OF
WESTERN EUROPE

To the memory of my friend the late
HUGH M. Le FLEMING

First published 1963

This impression 1976

ISBN 0 7110 0637 7

Published by Ian Allan Ltd, Shepperton, Surrey,
and printed in the United Kingdom by
Ian Allan Printing Ltd.

PREFACE

In this book I have tried to describe in words and pictures the last steam locomotives in Western Europe.

The transition from steam to other forms of motive power is a gradual process which is by no means synchronised between country and country, nor is its progress equally swift. For example, the last steam locomotives in Italy were designed in 1930 but steam is still (1962) at work in several parts of that country. On the other hand, Holland received new steam locomotives in 1946, but outside museums, no standard gauge steam now exists there.

Apart from some 2—10—0 locomotives being built in Turkey, steam locomotive construction for the major railways came to an end in Western Europe in 1961 with Garratt locomotives for the R.E.N.F.E. and the overall run-down of steam stock will obviously proceed at an increased rate as diesel and electric power form the complete replacement. In such countries as Turkey and Spain, however, some steam locomotives may well survive for another 50 years or more, while Germany will not see their complete disappearance until 1980.

For these reasons, in this book, any attempt to give firm dates for the periods of "the last of steam" in the different countries has been avoided. As, however, the replacement of steam is inevitable and progressive, descriptions have, for the sake of uniformity, all been written in the past tense.

No attempt has been made to list or to describe all the locomotives of any one country; the idea has rather been to show a representative selection of engines which could have been seen in each of the countries during the final years of steam working. As much information as possible has been given about the engines illustrated, though apart from considerations of space, the amount of detail available varies very greatly between country and country and this is reflected in the descriptions given. Naturally, most space has been given to those countries in which most steam locomotive development has occurred.

Great care has been taken to ensure accuracy of the details given and in most cases, at least two authorities have been consulted. Alas, in many instances there is far from complete agreement even about dimensions, dates and numbers, and in some cases the official information has been proven wrong. Where such conflict exists, I have relied upon my own knowledge and deduction to conclude which authority is probably correct.

The scope of the book covers locomotives of all the state-owned railways of broad or standard gauge, and the two most important state-owned metre-gauge lines. Two nominally privately owned standard gauge lines which are important public carriers are also included but the locomotives of privately-owned industrial railways are not covered. Narrow gauge locomotives are not mentioned, partly because they have already been excellently documented in two recent books: *Narrow Gauge Railways of Europe* (Ian Allan, 1959) and *Steam on the Sierra* (Cleaver Hume, 1960). Also excluded are all experimental and unconventional steam locomotives, which have been described recently in *The Concise Encyclopaedia of World Railway Locomotives* (Hutchinson, 1959).

"Western Europe" has been taken politically rather than geographically and such countries as Greece and the whole of Turkey (since it must be considered as one country) have been included. It has been my good fortune to visit the railways of all these Western European countries at least once, in the last ten years. In all of them I have been privileged to visit their installations and motive power depots, and in most I have been able to make considerable journeys on locomotive footplates. Thus I have been able not only to collect a vast amount of first-hand knowledge but also to take many photographs, of which a small selection are now presented. In only four instances have I been unable to illustrate noteworthy locomotives from my own collection and Messrs. Nydquist & Holm have very kindly supplied me with the originals for Plates 176, 177, 291 and 292 to fill the gaps.

HERNE BAY   P. R-W.
1962.

AUSTRIAN FEDERAL RAILWAYS
Österreichischen Bundesbahnen: O.B.B.

Gauge: 4ft 8½in (1.435m)

The O.B.B. also operates 340 miles of 29.9 in (760 mm) gauge subsidiary lines.

The first steam locomotives to run in Austria were two built by Robert Stephenson & Co., Newcastle upon Tyne, in 1837 for the Kaiser-Ferdinand-Nordbahn. They were of the 2—2—0 type with inside cylinders and were named *Austria* and *Moravia* respectively. *Austria* hauled the first train between Florisdorf and Deutsch-Wagram on 23rd November, 1837.

During the nineteenth and the early part of the twentieth centuries, Austrian locomotive design had a very great influence upon that of other Continental European railways. This was largely due to two great men, John Haswell and Karl Gölsdorf, each of whom was among the foremost locomotive engineers of his day.

John Haswell went to Austria from England with the first locomotives in 1837. He ultimately became manager of the Vienna Works of the State Railway and was responsible for many developments in locomotive design. He introduced the Stephenson valve gear to Austria, built the first six-coupled locomotive in 1846 and the first eight-coupled in 1851 for the Semmering trials. Fitted with a form of counter-pressure braking this latter engine was not entirely successful, but after modification it became the prototype of the 1855 0—8—0 design and the standard European mountain locomotive. Considerable side-play was allowed in the coupled axles.

Dr. Karl Gölsdorf was C.M.E. of the State Railways from 1893 until his death in 1916. He was responsible for 63 locomotive designs, including many two-cylinder and four-cylinder compounds with his simple automatic change valve. He designed his own valve gear, dispensing with expansion links.

Among the most outstanding of the Gölsdorf designs were the first European 0—10—0s, built in 1900—two-cylinder compounds with ample side-play in the coupled axles; the first compound 2—6—2s in Europe (1904); four-cylinder compound 2—10—0s (1906); the first locomotives of the 2—6—4 type—four-cylinder compounds introduced in 1908; and the first 2—12—0, in 1911. In 1912 came the 0—12—0 Abt rack and adhesion tank locomotives of Type 197 (Plate 20) for the Vordernberg line, and these, together with his two-cylinder simple and two-cylinder compound 2—6—2s of 1916 (Plates 2 and 3), were among the last survivors of steam in Austria.

The immediate "post-Gölsdorf" era was marked by the building between 1917 and 1922 of a hundred two-cylinder simple 2—8—0s of Type 156 (Plate 1).

After the First War came the carve-up of the Austro-Hungarian Empire and with it necessary modifications in locomotive designs. In 1923 the Austrian Federal Railways (O.B.B.) amalgamated the original State Railway with all the independent companies except the Südbahn which, however, was brought under State control in 1924.

The modern Austrian steam locomotive dates from the period 1922–1938 with Rihosek, Lehner and Emmerich Karner responsible for the designs. Apart from some two-cylinder compound 2—10—0s built in 1922 (Type 181), and a single three-cylinder 2—8—4 in 1928, all engines were two-cylinder simples, most of them were oscillating-cam Lentz valves operated by Walschaert valve gear. Outstanding designs were the ninety 2—10—0s of Type 81 (later Type 58) introduced in 1920, which became the standard heavy freight engines; the forty 4—8—0s of Type 113 (later Type 33) of 1923–1928 (Plate 5); and the 2—8—4s of Type 214 (later Type 12), of which the first appeared in 1928 (Plate 6). The single three-cylinder 2—8—4 was built for comparative trials with the two-cylinder design, but was never so satisfactory and was scrapped. Thirteen of these large engines were built between 1928 and 1936 for working on the Western main line. With the complete electrification of this line after the Second War, some were transferred to the Südbahn for work on the Semmering line to the Italian frontier. However, the 4—8—0s and the various post-war German 2—10—0s were well able to handle this traffic, and the 2—8—4s were withdrawn to store several years before the Südbahn main line was electrified. Attempts to sell the engines to Roumania, who had some of the same type, failed, and they were ultimately scrapped.

Several excellent tank engine designs made their appearance during the same period. For passenger work 4—6—2Ts and 4—6—4Ts were built. The former were a modernised and enlarged version of a 1917 Südbahn design; five were built in 1927 with Caprotti gear and 25 with Lentz O.C. valves (Plate 14). The 4—6—4Ts (Plate 15) were bigger engines altogether, again with Lentz O.C. valves. Sixteen were built in 1931–1936 at Florisdorf and a further ten in 1938–1939, after the German occupation. These last engines had several Reichsbahn characteristics, including inward-sloping cab sides.

In 1922 20 powerful 2—10—2Ts, Type 95 (Plate 16), were built, followed in 1928 by a further five. These engines were used extensively for assisting trains up the northern slopes of the Semmering. Then in 1927 appeared

1. Two-cylinder 2—8—0 No.156.3420 with a train for Vordernberg at Leoben.

two noteworthy standard designs, one a 2—8—2T, Type 93 (Plate 17) for freight and passenger branch line duties, the other an 0—8—0T, Type 392 (Plate 18) for heavy shunting. Fifty of the former type and 167 of the latter were constructed during the next four years and the superheated boiler, motion, axleboxes, tanks and many other details were the same for both, but as the 2—8—2T had less adhesion weight than the 0—8—0T it also had smaller cylinders and lighter main frames. All these engines had O.C. Lentz valves.

In 1935 an old State Railways 0—6—0T of 1898 was rebuilt into a 2—2—2 single-driver tank engine for light, high-speed branch-line work, with semi-automatic controls. Provision was made for automatic firing with either coal or oil. This locomotive was later further modified so that by adjusting the springs of the carrying wheels the load on the single driving axle could be varied (Plate 11). It was used by many European railways for bridge testing purposes.

Unusual engines were the twenty light and fast 2—4—2Ts with O.C. poppet valves, built 1935–37. Classed as *Dampftriebwagen* or steam railcars, they were oil-fired, had Heinl feed pumps and were intended for semi-automatic, one-man operation. A guard's and baggage compartment was provided on the engine, the guard being expected to assist the driver. They could haul 120 *tonnes* (say three bogie coaches), providing far greater capacity than the petrol railcars of the period. After the War, they were converted to coal burning and used on branch-line and local services.

After the Anschluss of 1938, the O.B.B. became part of the Deutsche Reichsbahn and from then on, new locomotives were of German standard types, mostly 2—10—0s of Types 42, 50 and, later, 52. Exceptions were two rack and adhesion 2—12—2Ts (Plate 22) and the additions to the 4—6—4Ts already noted.

The end of the Second War saw the O.B.B. again a separate organisation, but one which was so short of motive power that, for a few years, it had to use locomotives originating in fourteen different European countries.

During and immediately after the War many *Kriegslokomotiven* of D. R. Type 52 (Plates 218 and 312), and a smaller number of Type 42 (Plate 9) were built in Austria. Many were absorbed into O.B.B. stock, retaining their original numbers, excepting that locomotives of Type 52 with bar frames became Type 152 on the O.B.B. Survivors of both types were among the last of steam in Austria.

Of the many older German types which remained, the 2—8—2Ts of Type 86 (Plate 124) were active on freight and passenger trains on steeply graded secondary lines. Many of these engines were built at Florisdorf after 1938.

The outstanding post-war development in Austrian steam locomotive practice was the adoption of the multiple-jet oblong ejector evolved by Dr. Giesl-Gieslingen of Vienna Technical University. Experiments to improve the steaming of the boiler and the overall efficiency of the locomotive by modifying the blast were carried out on the 2—8—4 locomotives in 1928 and trials continued until the introduction of the first ejector in 1951. The ejector reduced back pressure, increased superheat and, by reducing the shock losses during the mixing of the gases and steam, utilised much more of the kinetic energy of the exhaust to do useful work. Giesl ejectors were fitted to locomotives in many countries the world over.

The future motive power policy on the O.B.B. is electrification of the main lines with single-phase A.C., 15kV, 16⅔ cycles. Diesel-electric locomotives and diesel-mechanical and diesel-hydraulic multiple-unit train sets and railcars will operate all secondary main lines and branch lines. This programme is near completion.

3

2. No. 135.313 was one of Gölsdorf's 2—6—2 two-cylinder compounds of 1911 design. They were followed by the two-cylinder simples of Type 35.

3. Two-cylinder simple 2—6—2 No. 35.214 with a train for Graz at Brück-a-d-Mur. Some of these engines had O.C. Lentz valves.

4. 4—6—0 No. 38.4103 at Amstetten with a train for Bischofshofen. These two-cylinder simples were built for the Südbahn in 1912-14, and some had Giesl ejectors.

5. 4—8—0 No 33.133 leaving the Haupt Tunnel at the summit of the Semmering Pass with an express from Italy to Vienna. These two-cylinder engines, with O.C. Lentz valves, acquired Giesl ejectors and German type smoke deflectors during their later years. They were displaced from the Süd main line by electrification.

6. 2—8—4 No. 12.10 on Vienna—Rome Express leaving Brück-a-d-Mur. This was the last of these fine engines in service and it was withdrawn before the Südbahn was electrified.

7. No. 157.414 was a Gölsdorf two-cylinder compound 0—10—0 of 1909. It had one of the enormous spark-arresting chimneys, nicknamed "bread baskets", which were necessary to prevent forest fires. In the mid-fifties, conventional stove pipe chimneys, Giesl ejectors and spark arresters could often be seen side-by-side, making a sight unique in steam locomotive history.

8. 2—10—0 No. 258.917 was a former Südbahn two-cylinder simple of Type 580 built between 1912 and 1922. Engines of this type were also built for Greece, where they were Class Lamda-Alpha (Plate 159), and others found their way to Italy after the first war, where they were Group 482 of the F.S. ▼

9. 2—10—0 No. 42.2337 was one of a batch built in Austria in 1945-47 but of a standard German heavy freight engine design. Twenty Austrian-built engines of this type went to Luxembourg (C.F.L. Type 55) and 33 others to Bulgaria (Type 16). Some of the O.B.B. engines displaced by electrification were sold to Hungary. The "Kabinentender" was a common feature of both German and Austrian heavy freight power in the last days of steam. It provided comfortable accommodation for freight train guards and did away with the need for a separate guard's van. As all Continental trains have continuous brakes a brake van, in the British sense, is not necessary.

10. 2—12—0 four-cylinder compound No. 659.23 was one of several Württemberg State Rys. Class K sent to Austria during the Second War to work freight over the Semmering. They ended their days as bankers on the south slopes of the Semmering from Mürzzu-schlag, No. 659.23 being the last survivor. The design dates from 1917, the builders being Esslingen, and it followed in several particulars the first-ever European twelve-coupler, the four-cylinder compound of Gölsdorf built in 1911. ▼

11. No. 69.02, a 2—2—2T used for bridge testing. The fuel oil tank is seen in front of the cab.

12. 2—4—2T No. 3071.20 on a local train in Styria.

13. Püchberg train about to leave Wiener Neustadt, with a two-cylinder compound 2—6—0T, No. 91.115 of the old State Railway. Engines of this type were built between 1897 and 1913.

8

14. 4—6—2T No. 77.261 was built in 1927 and was fitted with Lentz valves. It later had a Giesl ejector and water softening apparatus, the tank for which can be seen in front of the steam dome, the second dome being a sand-box.

15. 4—6—4T No. 78.614 was one of the original 1931-1936 series, later fitted with the Giesl ejector. The sensible length of the fill-hole in the tanks, a feature strange to British practice, can be judged by the length of the open fill-hole cover seen in the picture. It will also be noticed that the water column has no bag. ▼

9

16. 2—10—2T No. 95.109 with Lentz valves, Giesl ejector and smoke deflectors.

17. 2—8—2T No. 93.1384. Note the ash chute and small door in bottom of smoke-box to avoid the need to open the smoke-box door.

18. 0—8—0T No. 392.2510, many parts of which are interchangeable with Type 93 (above).

19. In Austria, iron ore is quarried out of the side of a mountain and is then carried by rail in hopper wagons, mostly to the blast furnaces at Donawitz. The route followed by the iron-ore trains is over a steeply graded section of the former State Railways line from Leoben to Reisling. Between Vordernberg and Eisenerz, much of the line has a ruling gradient of 1 in 15, and such sections are rack-operated on the Abt system. Three types of non-compound rack and adhesion tank locomotives were built for the line; the loco-motives each consisted of two separate two-cylinder engines, one driving the adhesion wheels and the other the cogged rack-wheels. They received steam from the same boiler, but there were separate regulators. Seen above is one of 18 0—6—2T built between 1890 and 1908 heading a train of empty hoppers on a rack section near Prebischl. The train was banked by an 0—12—0T (Plate 20). The future motive power for this line is diesel-electric rack and adhesion locomotives.

20. No. 197.301—one of the three Gölsdorf rack and adhesion 0—12—0T. The tail rods, cylinder covers and valve covers of the rack engine are clearly seen. Considerable side play was arranged in the 1st, 5th and 6th axles.

21. View showing the arrangement of inside (rack) and outside (adhesion) cylinders and motion in Type 297.

22. No. 297.401, one of two rack and adhesion 2—12—2T built in 1941 under Deutsche Reichsbahn direction.

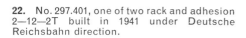

Graz—Koflacher Eisenbahn: G.K.B.

Gauge: 4ft 8½in (1.435m)

The G.K.B. began its long life in 1860 as a colliery line to carry soft brown coal from the open-cast mines at Köflach to the main line of the Austrian Südbahn at Graz. In 1873 a line was built from Lieboch to Wies-Eibiswald to exploit coal and other mineral deposits, and in 1930 the small Sülmtalbahn was amalgamated with the G.K.B. The Südbahn operated the G.K.B. for 50 years, until 1924, when the railway's finances improved sufficiently for it again to become independent. To-day the G.K.B. forms a part of the nationalised Alpine-Montan mining combine.

The steam locomotive stock consisted entirely of old engines of the former Austrian State Railways and the Südbahn. The standard freight engines were 2—8—0 two-cylinder compounds of Type 56 (formerly Type 170) built between 1914 and 1918 for the State Railways (Plate 25) and the passenger locomotives were 4—4—0s built 1890–1897 as Südbahn Type 17c (Plate 24); ex-Süd Type 32d-1 0—6—0Ts (Plate 26) and two-cylinder compound 2—6—2Ts (Plate 27) were used for shunting. For longevity, pride of place was taken by four 0—6—0s (ex-Südbahn Type 29), each of which was over 100 years old (Plate 23). These engines were built at the Vienna Works of the State Railway and the original builders' plates were engraved "J. HASWELL (Director)".

The future motive power of the G.K.B. will probably remain steam for freight, but Uerdingen rail buses and trailers are taking over all passenger services.

23. 0—6—0 No. 671, built in 1860 as Südbahn Type 29. At Lieboch.

24. 4—4—0 No. 409 ex-Südbahn Type 17c (1890-97) with the evening train from Graz to Köflach. These engines had one water gauge and three try-cocks, which were used regularly. The cabs were large and comfortable and at their maximum permitted speed of 50 m.p.h. these excellent old engines rode very well.

25. Nos. 56.3147 and 56.3279 at the head of a freight train at Graz. These were two-cylinder compound 2—8—0s ex-State Railways Type 170 built between 1914 and 1919. The low pressure side is shown here. The spark arresters with which many were fitted were later removed and most of the sixteen engines had new chimneys like that on No. 56.3279 below, but some had Giesl ejectors. All of them retained their Clench steam driers.

26. 0—6—0T No. 1851 ex-Süd Type 32d-1 of 1898; shunting at Köflach. Notice the steel "props" supporting the chimney and the safety valves.

27. This two-cylinder compound 2—6—2T was No. 1 of the Sülmtalbahn and was No. 30.103 of the State Railways, built in 1899. This photograph shows the high pressure side.

BELGIAN NATIONAL RAILWAYS COMPANY

Société National des Chemins de Fer Belges: S.N.C.B.

Gauge: 4ft 8½in (1.435m)

This Company was formed in 1926 to take over the State Railways administration and operation. It owns all the standard gauge lines in the country.

The first railway to operate on the Continent of Europe was that between Brussels and Malines in Belgium. Three locomotives were present at the opening ceremony on 5th May, 1835, two inside-cylinder 2—2—2s built by Robert Stephenson & Co. and named *La Flèche* and *Stephenson*, and one inside-cylinder 0—4—2, *L'Eléphant*, built by Tayleur & Co. *La Flèche* hauled the first train.

In the nineteenth century the Belgian State Railways had two world-famous engineers, Alfred Belpaire and Egide Walschaert. Belpaire, who between 1864 and 1893 was first C.M.E. and then President of the State Railways, designed the flat-topped firebox with shallow, sloping grate which bears his name. Walschaert, who was locomotive foreman at Brussels-Midi depot, invented the radial valve gear which has found world-wide application.

In the early years of this century another eminent C.M.E. was J. B. Flamme, who designed the large and powerful four-cylinder 2—10—0s of Type 36 and the equally large Pacifics of Type 10 (Plate 28), both of which were introduced in 1909-10. The 2—10—0s were all superseded soon after the Second War by German 2—10—0s but many of the 4—6—2s lasted until the late nineteen-fifties.

In 1935 there appeared the first of 35 four-cylinder Pacifics of Type 1 (Plate 29) and these engines superseded the Type 10 on most important express trains. Six remarkable 4—4—2 locomotives of Type 12 (Plate 30) were put into service in 1938, and these proved to be the last express engines to be built for the S.N.C.B.

For secondary passenger services, four-cylinder de Glehn compound 4—6—0s of Type 7 (Plate 32) were late survivors of steam. They were 1934 rebuilds of Type 8bis built 1919-20. Many had double blast-pipes and chimneys.

For freight and mixed traffic duties the Belgians always favoured the 2—8—0 tender engine and in 1921-22 Armstrong Whitworth built a large number of two-cylinder Consolidations with plate frames. These were Type 37, all of which were rebuilt from 1936 to become Type 31 (Plate 35). Also in 1921, Baldwin and Alco delivered 150 2—8—0s with bar frames but with otherwise similar dimensions. These were Type 38 (Plate 36). After the Second War, the Belgian Railways were largely revitalised by no fewer than 300 2—8—0s obtained during 1945-47 from Alco and Canadian builders. These were Type 29 (Plate 37).

Curious and persistent relics of the age of steam were the 0—6—0s and 4—4—2Ts of McIntosh Caledonian ancestry. These engines, Type 41 and Type 15 respectively (Plates 38 and 39), were survivors of the 1898-1913 period during which the State Railways purchased 0—6—0s (more than 500 of these!) 4—4—0s, 4—6—0s and 4—4—2 tanks all of which were identical with, or developed from, the current McIntosh designs for the Caledonian Railway.

Of the S.N.C.B. 0—6—0 and 0—8—0 shunting tanks, the former were outside-framed panniers of Type 51 (Plate 40) which first appeared in 1866. The 0—8—0Ts of Type 53 (Plate 42), of which nearly 400 were built, first appeared in 1904 and were of a simple, straight-forward design.

As a result of German occupation in both world wars, Belgium had a large number of locomotives of German origin, particularly those left as reparations after 1918. Prussian types were predominant, the S-10 (Plate 34) and S-10/2 4—6—0s being the principal express locomotives and the P-8 4—6—0s (Plate 33) and their freight version, the G-8/1 0—8—0s (Plate 46), being by far the most numerous. Tank engines of Prussian Types T-9 (Plate 44), T-12 (Plate 123), T-14 (Plate 122) and T-16 (Plate 45) were other late survivors of steam.

Other World War I relics to remain until the last days of steam were American locomotives built in 1917-18 (mostly by Baldwin) for the British Military Railways in France and sold to the Belgians at the end of hostilities. These were 0—6—0Ts of Type 58 (Plate 41), 2—6—2Ts of Type 57 (Plate 43) and 4—6—0s of Type 40 (Plate 31).

From the Second War two principal German types emerged, both 2—10—0s. Thirteen D.R. Type 50 were S.N.C.B. Type 25 (Plate 47) and 90 D.R. Type 52 became Type 26. These engines, together with 2—8—0s of Type 29, displaced both the Flamme 2—10—0s and the four large, highly unsuccessful 2—8—2s of Type 5 (1929) from all heavy freight duties, especially the mineral traffic on the Luxembourg line.

The future motive power of the S.N.C.B. is electric on most of the main lines, current being taken from overhead conductors at 3,000 volts D.C. Diesel-electric locomotives work both passenger and freight on non-electrified main lines, and diesel railcars and railbuses are much in evidence for secondary passenger services.

16

28. Four-cylinder 4—6—2 No. 10.010, one of the first batch (1910-12) of Flamme Pacifics. The second batch (1912-14) had smaller grates and modified weight distribution. Both batches were rebuilt by F. Legein (then C.M.E.) from 1922. Larger superheaters and Kylchap blast pipes with double chimneys were fitted. The "platform" in front of the smoke-box covered the inside cylinders, which were placed well forward in order to drive the leading coupled axle. The outside valve gear drove the inside valves through rocking shafts, the drive being taken from the front of the outside valve spindle.

29. Four-cylinder 4—6—2 No. 1.016 with an Amsterdam to Paris express at Mons. These Type 1 Pacifics had bar frames and the inside cylinders drove the leading coupled axle, the drive to the inside valves being similar to that of Type 10. The streamlined casing was similar to that of Gresley's 2—8—2 *Cock o'the North* in its original form. Type 1 was the last heavy express locomotive design for the S.N.C.B., the only later express locomotives being the much smaller Atlantics of Type 12.

30. 4—4—2 No. 12.003 leaving Lille with a train for Tournai. These remarkable machines were intended to work light, fast trains, mostly between Brussels and Ostend. They were streamlined on the Huet principles of air-smoothing, but none the less, all revolving and reciprocating parts were easily accessible. They had bar frames and inside cylinders with Walschaert valve gear, the return cranks for which were driven from the outside crank-pin of the leading coupled wheels. One of the class had Caprotti valves.

31. 4—6—0 No. 40.020 with a train for Tournai at Mons. These Baldwin 4—6—0s dated from 1917. They had bar frames which, no doubt, accounted for their longevity. At least two acquired Giesl ejectors.

32. Four cylinder compound 4—6—0 No. 7.053 with double blast-pipe and chimney and A.C.F.1 feed water pump and heater. Two of this class had the four cylinders in line.

33. 4—6—0 No. 64.136, ex-Prussian Class P-8. This engine had an exhaust steam ejector and there were several minor differences as a result of Belgian ownership.

34. Four cylinder simple 4—6—0 No. 60.013, ex-Prussian Class S-10. The S.N.C.B also had a few four-cylinder compounds of Class S-10/2. ▼

▲**35.** Rebuilt Armstrong-Whitworth 2—8—0 No. 31.088 on a Bruges-Brussels fast train near Aalter.

36. American-built 2—8—0 No. 38.099 of 1921.

37. Canadian-built 2—8—0 No. 29.177, introduced after the Second War.

20

38. Superheater 0—6—0 No. 41.195 of the "McIntosh era". The wing plates were typically Caledonian.

39. If McIntosh had designed a 4—4—2T it would probably have looked like this non-superheater engine, No. 15.001, seen at Walcourt on a Vireux-Walcourt train. The chimney capuchon was hinged and its position was reversed for bunker-first running.

40. 0—6—0PT No. 51.024. Introduced **1866,** these little tanks were built in batches over the next 40 years, older engines being scrapped as they wore out. They had their counterparts in the 0—6—0PTs of the **Great Western Railway in England.**

41. 0—6—0T No. 58.027, built by Baldwin, 1917-8, for the British Military Railways in France.

42. Standard 0—8—0T No. 53.372.

43. Baldwin 2—6—2ST No. 57.039.

▲**44.** 2—6—0T No. 93.065, ex-Prussian Class T—9/3.

45. 0—10—0T No. 98.008, ex-Prussian Class T—16, used for banking up the 1 in 39½ from Liege (Guillemins) until the coming of electrification.

46. Freight train near Hasselt with 0—8—0 No. 81.539, ex Prussian Class G—8/1. This was the most numerous class on the S.N.C.B., 582 being in service after the Second War.

47. Of a German wartime order for 200 D.R. 2—10—0 Type 50 locomotives built in Belgium, thirteen were not completed at the Liberation, and these, of which No. 25.010 was one, became S.N.C.B. Type 25. The rest were scrapped later in Germany, except 12 which went to Denmark to become D.S.B. Class N.

DANISH STATE RAILWAYS

Danske Statsbaner: D.S.B.

Gauge : 4ft 8½in (1.435m)

The State Railways own and operate the principal lines in Denmark, though there are many small, privately owned railways which operate some 40 per cent of the total railway mileage of the nation.

The first locomotive to run in Denmark was an inside-cylinder 2—2—2 named *Odin*, one of five built in 1846 by Sharp Bros., of Manchester, for the Zealand Railway (Copenhagen to Roskilde) and now part of the State Railways. *Odin* was one of the standard "Sharp Singles" which were supplied to many countries.

Denmark is predominantly a flat country and the D.S.B. have never owned any very large or powerful locomotives. Small 4—4—0s (Plates 48 and 49) and 2—6—0s (Plate 52) remained on active service well into the era of the last days of steam. The largest passenger locomotives were compound Pacifics originally bought from the Swedish State Railways (Plate 54) though others of the same design were built in Denmark later (Plate 55).

The largest Danish-designed freight engines were the three-cylinder 2—8—0s of Class H (Plate 56) and the largest freight tank engines were 0—8—0Ts of Class Q for service in the marshalling yards and on the humps. The smallest engines in recent service were the diminutive 0—4—0Ts of Class HS.

From the several private railways absorbed by the State the only important locomotives taken over were three typical 2—8—2Ts built by Henschel in 1917, one for the South Funen Railway and two for the Svendborg-Faaborg Railway. These three engines became D.S.B. Class DF.

The Danish Railways had fewer ex-German locomotives after the Second War than had most other countries in Europe. Twelve 2—10—0s of D.R. Type 50 (Plate 47) built in Belgium in 1943 and sold by Germany to Denmark in 1948 became D.S.B. Class N and three Prussian Class P-8 4—6—0s (Plates 33 and 118) became D.S.B. Class T.

Danish steam locomotives could always be recognised by the metal "cuff" carrying the national red-white-red colours and fixed around the chimneys. In common with other Scandinavian locomotives, those of the D.S.B. had the sand-box immediately in front of the steam dome and under the same cover.

All the compound locomotives were of the balanced type and had a large common piston valve for each pair of cylinders. In the case of three-cylinder simple engines (Classes H, R-II, R-III and S) the eccentric drive for the inside Heusinger valve gear was taken from a return crank combined with that for the L.H. outside valve. A large number of smaller engines, 2—4—0, 4—4—0 and especially the prolific 0—6—0Ts of Class F, had outside link motion of the Allan (or Tricks) straight-link type.

The D.S.B. made extensive use of hollow firebox stays and this feature was obvious in many classes. In those locomotives not equipped with electric lighting the acetylene-gas bottle on the running plate was a characteristic feature.

The steam locomotive in Denmark was always at a disadvantage for two reasons. First, there is no coal in Denmark and imported coal is very expensive. Second, fresh water in Denmark is almost universally very hard, resulting in very high boiler maintenance costs. "Softener bricks" in the tender helped to reduce the damage but caused severe priming, necessitating continuous blowing down, and the blown-down scum caused corrosion of the steel sleepers widely used on the D.S.B.

The future of Danish motive power is diesel-electric locomotives, which were first used on the D.S.B. in 1927. Various forms of diesel multiple-unit trains and railcars have also been in service for many years, perhaps the most famous being the high-speed Lyntog diesel m-u. trains of 1935.

The only electrification in Denmark is that of the Copenhagen suburban area, which uses 1,500 volts D.C. with overhead conductors.

48. 4—4—0 No. 719 Class C with a boat train at Copenhagen Ferryport. Five of these engines were built by Esslingen in 1903 and fourteen by Schwartzkopff in 1909. All were later superheated.

49. Rebuilt 4—4—0 No. 566 Class K-2 coaling at Dybbolsbro shed, Copenhagen. Class K originated in 1894 with five engines from Neilson & Co. and during the next eight years a further 95 were supplied by German and Italian builders. Between 1925 and 1932 many were rebuilt to Class K-2 in the D.S.B. shops at Copenhagen and Aarhus with superheater boilers and piston valves but retaining the original outside Allan link motion.

50 and 51. 4—4—2 No. 912 Class P-1. These beautiful machines were four-cylinder balanced compounds with a common piston valve for each pair of cylinders, and with Heusinger valve gear inside the frames. Nineteen engines were built at Linden in 1907-9 and a further fourteen with larger cylinders and higher boiler pressure came from Schwartzkopff in 1910 (Class P-2). Between 1943 and 1955 a number of both series were rebuilt at Copenhagen as light Pacifics, Class PR. The bar frames of the original were extended backwards and the boiler lengthened by an extra ring. A new firebox standard with that of Class R was fitted but cylinders and motion remained unaltered. The six coupled wheels were 5 ft 8 in against the 6 ft 6 in of the Atlantics. No. 908 is shown below.

52. 2—6—0 No. 894 Class D-2 with a local train at Esbjerg. The 2—6—0 was for many years the standard type for branch lines and four similar classes were built between 1902 and 1912, the axle-load of the heaviest being only 13 *tonnes*. All were superheated.

53. Three-cylinder 4—6—0 No. 956 Class R-II with an express at Aalborg. These engines were obviously similar to the Prussian S-10/2. They were built by Borsig in 1921. Frichs built another lot in 1924 and these were Class R-III. Engines similar in appearance but with two cylinders were known as Class R-I.

54 and 55. Four-cylinder compound 4—6—2 No. 968 Class E. The largest express locomotives of the D.S.B. were eleven Pacifics, Nos. 964—974, bought in 1936 from the Swedish State Railways, where they had become redundant as a result of electrification. They were balanced compounds with common piston valves for each pair of cylinders and were built by Nydquist & Holm between 1914 and 1916. A change valve admitted live steam at reduced pressure to the low pressure cylinders. Between 1943 and 1947 a further 25 engines were built by Frichs to the same designs but incorporating improvements to the grate and the cab and providing an extra "dry steam" dome. Several had double blast-pipes and chimneys. No. 984 of this later series is shown below.

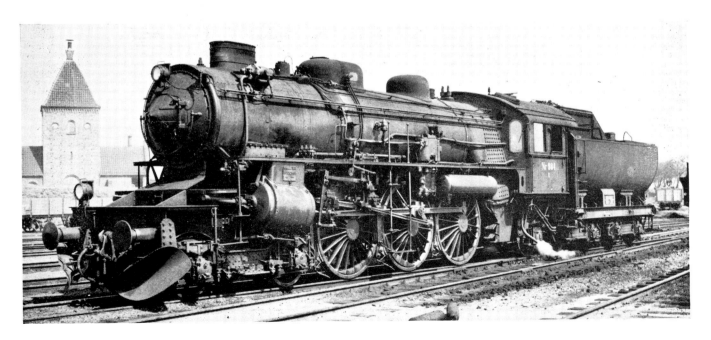

C

▲56. Three-cylinder 2—8—0 No. 791 Class H, showing the double
return crank on the crank pin of the third left coupled wheel. Built
by Frichs 1923-26. A later series came out in 1941.

57. From the foot-
plate of a Class H
2—8—0 an imposing
view was obtained
of an ex-Swedish
Pacific on a train
near Vejle.

58. 0—6—0T No. 673 Class F. One of a large number of similar engines built between 1898 and 1949 and used extensively for shunting.

59. 0—8—0T No. 342 Class Q. The standard heavy shunting engine of the D.S.B., built between 1930 and 1945.

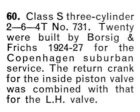

60. Class S three-cylinder 2—6—4T No. 731. Twenty were built by Borsig & Frichs 1924-27 for the Copenhagen suburban service. The return crank for the inside piston valve was combined with that for the L.H. valve.

FINNISH STATE RAILWAYS

Valtionrautatiet: V.R.

Gauge : 5ft 0in (1.524m)

The rail gauge is the same as that of the U.S.S.R, as Finland achieved independence from Russia only in 1917.

The first locomotive in Finland, an outside-cylinder 4—4—0 named *Ilmarinen*, was built by the Canada Works, Birkenhead, as their No. 83 of 1860. This locomotive opened the first railway in Finland on March 17th, 1862, between Helsinki and Hameenlinna.

During the last days of steam the locomotives of the V.R. were strongly built, two-cylinder simple designs, there being no multi-cylinder or compound engines. All the later types had bar frames and all engines had piston valves, often with cylinder by-pass valves.

Boilers had round-top fireboxes, and even those for the smaller types had superheaters. They were usually fed by 2 Friedmann injectors, one of which was of the exhaust steam type on main-line engines. The firehole doors were air-operated, with a pedal awkwardly placed for the uninitiated, in the centre of the footplate. Sand boxes were on top of the boiler but only on the 4—6—2s, 2—8—2s and 2—10—0s were they incorporated in the dome cover.

Cow-catchers were fitted as the track is unfenced and much of the route mileage is through forest. Small snow-ploughs could be fitted over the cow-catchers in the winter. All the locomotives had an air-operated bell, used in the vicinity of stations or goods yards, and two different-toned whistles, a high-tone whistle used as a warning in the conventional way, and a low-toned whistle used only when brakes were tested, or applied in an emergency (including a signal check) and when shunting.

Most steam locomotives had electric lighting, but a few used acetylene gas, the bottle for which was carried on the running plate.

There is a simple system of locomotive classification: the first letter, a capital, indicates the type of locomotive. H—Passenger tender. T—Freight tender. S—Mixed traffic tender. P—Passenger tank, and V—Freight or shunting tank. The next letter is small and indicates the axle loading: k—under 11 *tonnes*. v—11 to 14 *tonnes*. r—over 14 *tonnes*. The figure following indicates roughly the age of the locomotive, 1 being the oldest group in service. So Class Tv-1 was a freight tender engine with an axle load between 11 and 14 *tonnes* and of the first group of such locomotives to be built. Tv-2 were introduced at a later date and so on. This system is used also for diesel locomotives.

Although track renewal on a grand scale is being carried out, much of the V.R. mileage is still laid with very light rail and the largest group of locomotives were 140 quite modern little 2—8—0s of Class Tk-3.

After the Second War, Finland received 20 2—10—0s, Class Tr-2 by Alco and Baldwin and part of a large order for Russia. The only other "reparations" engines were four 4—6—4Ts built by Henschel for Estonia and after the defeat of Germany sent to Helsinki for the suburban services. These engines, Class Pr-2, were non-standard and when the firebox crown collapsed in one of them, killing the men, they were withdrawn.

Coal has, in the past, been very scarce in Finland, and all of it has to be imported. A large number of locomotives have, therefore, been wood-burners. Birch logs about 2½ft long were used for fuel, hand-fired, two at a time, the firemen wearing special gloves. Compressed peat has also been used successfully.

Soft brown coal from Russia later became plentiful and proved to be good, if smoky, locomotive fuel. Considerable numbers of wood-burners were, however, still in service at a late date, and it is said that although no longer economical, they were kept as a form of government subsidy to the timber industry.

The future motive power for the V.R. is diesel-electric and diesel-hydraulic locomotives; a few diesel-mechanical "motor coach" locomotives with Wilson gearboxes are in service. Diesel-mechanical railcars with trailers are rapidly monopolising all branch line and suburban duties. There is no railway electrification at present.

61. No. 749 Class Hv-4 came from a class of smaller 4—6—0 passenger engines built between 1912 and 1933 in Tampere. This example had electric lighting and an exhaust steam injector and burned wood. The large spark-arresting chimney contained blades, so arranged that a vortex was induced in the exhaust, and sparks were extinguished before leaving the chimney.

62. No. 583 Class Hv-2. The largest of the seven 4—6—0 classes. Hv-2 and Hv-3 were identical except that the latter had eight-wheeled tenders of higher capacity than the six-wheeled type of Hv-2. Engines of these classes were built between 1919 and 1941 by German and Finnish builders. The cylinder by-pass valves, the air-operated bell in front of the cab, and the turbo-generator on the boiler were typical V.R. steam locomotive practice.

▲ **63.** 4—6—2 No. 1008 Class Hr-1 on Helsinki-Kouvola express near Pasila. The pointed board on the left indicates a permanent speed restriction.

The 22 Hr-1 Pacifics were the largest and latest (1937-1957) passenger steam locomotives. The most recent of them had pressure equalising piston valves in place of the by-pass valves and this was true also of the 2—8—2s of Class Tr-1 (Plate 65). The boilers, interchangeable with those of Class Tr-1, had two circulating tubes in the firebox and the later examples had welded steel fireboxes. They were hand-fired and steamed very freely. Wire-mesh spark arresters were fitted over the chimney top but some had the spark arrester at the base of the chimney petticoat. Both the Pacifics and the Mikados had bar frames and bogie tenders.

The 67 2—8—2s built between 1940 and 1957 were expected to be the last main-line steam engines to run in Finland. Although classed as freight engines, they were used largely for mixed traffic duties. They had a leading truck of the Krauss Helmholtz type and a trailing Adams truck. The last batch had roller bearings on all axles and connecting rod big ends, and modern German type smoke deflectors.

64. The fireman's view ahead from the footplate of a Mikado at speed.

34

65. 2—8—2 No. 1056 Class Tr–1 with a slow train from Helsinki to Riihimaki at Hyvinkaa.

66. American built 2—10—0 No. 1305 Class Tr–2. These engines had four circulating tubes in the firebox, and were stoker fired. The middle coupled wheels were flangeless.

67. 2—8—0 Class Tk-3 built between 1928 and 1950 in Finland and Denmark (Frichs). No. 873 was a wood-burner and the picture shows the fuelling shed at Turku. A stack of sawn birch logs is in the left foreground. This engine used acetylene gas lighting and the gas bottle can be seen on the running plate. Also clearly shown is the ash-chute below the smoke-box, which avoided the need to open the smoke-box door for cleaning; this was a standard feature of all V.R. steam locomotives.

68. A coal-burning 2—8—0 of Class Tk-3 No. 898 on a local passenger train about to leave Helsinki. This engine had electric lighting. ▼

▲ **69.** 2—8—0 No. 1207 of Class Tv-1, the second largest class on the V.R. 129 engines were built in Germany, Sweden and Finland between 1917 and 1928.

▲ **70.** Many 2—8—0s of Class Tv-1 burned wood, the tender being stacked high with 13 cubic metres of birch logs. Apart from the spark arresting chimney the main modification for wood-burning was the removal of the brick-arch in the firebox.

◄ **71.** The driver's view on a Class Tv-1 wood-burner.

37

72. The V.R. had five heavy 0—10—0T yard shunters of Class Vr-3, one built in Germany in 1924 and four in Finland in 1926. The boiler, cylinders and motion were interchangeable with those of the 2—8—2 suburban tank engines of Class Pr-1, sixteen of which were supplied contemporaneously by the same builders. Note the radio-telephone aerial on the top of the cab.

73. 2—8—2T No. 765 Class Pr-1 leaving Pasila with a suburban train for Helsinki.

74. Two standard 0—6—0T, Nos. 664 and 656 Class Vr-1 (1913-1927).

75. 0—6—2T No. 964 with spark-arresting chimney but burning coal. Class Vr-2 were built by Tampereen in 1930-31.

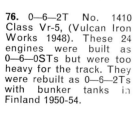

76. 0—6—2T No. 1410 Class Vr-5, (Vulcan Iron Works 1948). These 24 engines were built as 0—6—0STs but were too heavy for the track. They were rebuilt as 0—6—2Ts with bunker tanks in Finland 1950-54.

FRENCH NATIONAL RAILWAYS SOCIETY
Société Nationale des Chemins de Fer Français: S.N.C.F.

Gauge: 4ft 8½in (1.435m)

The S.N.C.F. came into being on 1st January, 1938, and took over the operation and control of all main-line companies, including that of the State Railway, which was itself the result of a 1909 amalgamation of the Ouest and the Réseau de l'Etat.

The first steam locomotive in France was an 0—4—0 built in 1828 by Robert Stephenson & Co. for the Lyon–St. Etienne Railway.

When one thinks of French steam locomotives one almost invariably thinks of four-cylinder compounds. Although by no means all French designs were compounds, it is fair to say that nowhere else in the world was the compound locomotive so highly developed or so widely used.

The first French compound was designed by an English-born engineer named Alfred de Glehn and built for the Nord Railway in 1886. Closely associated with de Glehn, who was chief engineer of the Société Alsacienne, was Gaston du Bousquet, who became C.M.E. of the Nord in 1890, and between them, these men were responsible for the highly successful development of a four-cylinder compound system which was applied to locomotives of many types, not only in France but in countries all over the world.

One of the most important steps in steam locomotive design was taken in July 1907, when the Société Alsacienne completed the first European Pacific, a four-cylinder de Glehn compound for the Paris–Orléans Railway to the requirements of M. Solacroup, the C.M.E. of the railway. With the exception of the Est, all the railways of France followed the lead of the P–O, and the compound Pacific became for many years the standard French express locomotive. Many different systems were used, and the Pacifics of the P.L.M. and the Collin Super-Pacifics of the Nord were particularly fine engines.

Another noteworthy "First" for France was the introduction in 1925 of the first 4—8—2 in Europe by the Chemin de Fer de l'Est. It was followed within a few weeks by a P.L.M. engine of the same type.

Both engines were four-cylinder compounds but were very different in design and appearance. In the P.L.M., engines the outside L.P. cylinders drove the leading coupled axle, while the inside H.P. cylinders drove the second axle. "Parabaloid" smoke box doors gave them a very dashing appearance. They were all modified during the nineteen-thirties and forties but one was built in 1931 with the inside H.P. cylinders driving the third coupled axle, and the L.P. cylinders the second. It also had larger driving wheels and a higher working pressure but smaller H.P. cylinders. This was No. 241. C.I, and by the mid-1950s it was the sole survivor of the P.L.M. Mountains. The Est Mountains lasted much longer and one is illustrated and described in Plate 84.

A great advance in locomotive design was made in 1929 when M. André Chapelon, C.M.E., of the P–O Railway, rebuilt one of the early Pacifics of that railway and, with a thorough understanding of the properties of steam and compounding, doubled its power output (Plate 79). Further similar reconstructions were equally successful and the most sensational results were obtained from the conversion of a Pacific to a 4—8—0 embodying the same principles of ample steam passages, poppet valves and double blast-pipes of the Kylchap type.

Chapelon, who had many inventions to his credit, became Chief of the Department of Locomotive Studies of the S.N.C.F., and as such was responsible for steam locomotive development in France from 1938 until his retirement in 1953. It was the greatest misfortune that at the height of his powers and influence, Europe was plunged into the Second War. Even so, he was undoubtedly the greatest locomotive engineer of our time and his influence on steam locomotive design was felt throughout the world.

With the great ability and authority of Chapelon it is sometimes forgotten that the French Railways were served by many other very able and brilliant locomotive men, among whom must be mentioned M. R. Vallantin, who was responsible for the initial rebuilding of the P.L.M. Pacifics on principles parallel to those of Chapelon, and whose 2—10—2 locomotives (Plate 86) were among the most outstanding machines of their day. Another very capable engineer was M. de Caso, the last C.M.E. of the Nord, whose 4—6—4 designs (Plate 81) were of such great interest.

Where existing classes of locomotives had proved satisfactory, they were, when necessary, multiplied by Chapelon with usually only slight modifications to enable some parts (e.g. smokebox doors) to be standardised. Such examples are the 2—10—0s of Series 150.P. (Plate 92) and the 2—10—2T of Series 151.TQ. (Plate 102).

The wide use of Pacifics for express passenger duties found its counterpart in the 2—8—2 Mikado design for fast freight and mixed-traffic duties, and all the old companies except the Est and the Midi owned locomotives of this type. The S.N.C.F. made great use of Mikados of two designs, first the four-cylinder compounds of Series 141.P. (Plate 90).

and secondly the tough post-War American-built engines of Series 141.R. (Plate 88). These engines were among the last French steam locomotives.

For general freight work, 2—8—os found most favour, both compounds and simples being built in large numbers for all the original companies. Compound 2—10—os were used by the Nord and the P.–O.–Midi, and three-cylinder simples by the Est (Plate 94) and the Etat, who had ten similar engines. The design was based on that of the Prussian Type G–12 (Plate 93), of which the Est inherited a large number after the First War. As a result of the Second War, three-cylinder 2—10—os of the German Type 44 (Plate 114) were built in Germany and France between 1944 and 1948. Known as Series 150.X., they were used on the heavy mineral trains of the Est Region, which received 139; the Nord got 39. After the electrification of these mineral lines some of the 150.X. were sold to Turkey (Plate 304).

In company with other European countries, France received large numbers of other German locomotives after both wars, including the usual Prussian types. The P–O also obtained two-cylinder bar-framed Pacifics and Mikados from America after the First War, and the S.N.C.F. the Series 141.R., already mentioned, after the Second War.

The furthest development in French steam locomotive design was reached in four types, all of them compounds.

First there was the compound six-cylinder 2—12—0, officially a 1940 reconstruction of a P–O–Midi 2—10—0 of 1912. This locomotive may be classed as a multi-cylinder experimental machine and does not properly come within the scope of this book, though it was a conventional design in many respects.

Second was the three-cylinder compound 4—8—4 No. 242.A.I (Plate 85), again a reconstruction, this time of a single unsuccessful three-cylinder simple 4—8—2 built for the Etat in 1932. This great engine did comparatively little work as its enormous power made balancing turns with smaller engines operationally difficult. If electrification had not progressed so fast there would doubtless have been many other examples of similar type.

Third was the four-cylinder compound of the Nord Region (Plate 82) No. 232.U.I, which gave ample evidence of its greatness and is considered by many to have been the most outstanding French steam locomotive of all time. As it is, No. 242.A.I and No. 232.U.I will be remembered, as will our own *Duke of Gloucester* and the German Type 10, the unfulfilled promises of what might have been.

Lastly come the 35 four-cylinder compound 4—8—2s of Series 241.P. (Plate 83) built between 1948 and 1952. The design was basically that of the rebuilt P.L.M. 4—8—2 No. 241.C.I. The new engines were always splendid machines, riding well, and being very economical in service. As in all the French compounds, provision was made to admit live steam, at reduced pressure, to the L.P. cylinders for starting.

What gave the French compounds their great success? The answer is undoubtedly that the credit goes as much to the very highly-trained enginemen as to their engines. Essential also to their success was the policy of allocating one engine to one driver, very often for many years at a stretch. The pride of "ownership" inherent in this system of "machine titulaire" is something that will never be seen on the railway again. It is significant that the majority of the last remaining steam locomotives in France, when most were in common-user service, were simple 2—8—2s and 2—8—os and that on the few regular compound duties the old system of one man, one engine was adhered to as far as possible.

The future motive power on French Railways will be electric on all main lines. Electrification of lines north of a line Bâle–Paris–Cherbourg will be monophase 50-cycle A.C., at 25kV. South of this line it is 1,500 volts D.C., with overhead conduction, though there are some short A.C. lines in the South and in the West the extension of electrification from Le Mans is to be A.C. Diesel-electric locomotives are used for main-line passenger and freight haulage on secondary lines and extensive use is made of diesel railcars and high-speed diesel train sets.

77. Four-cylinder compound 4—6—2 No. 231.K.47, ex-P.L.M., working a fast freight on the Nord Region, southbound through Pont de Briques. These engines had four cylinders in line, the H.P. being outside the frames. They were 1939-49 rebuilds of the 1909-21 series 231.C. and had independent cut-off for H.P. and L.P. cylinders. In series 231.D. and 231.F. which were rebuilt to 231.G., the cut-off could not be varied between H.P. and L.P. cylinders. Rebuilding of both series consisted of improving the steam passages, often with cylinder renewals, and fitting P.L.M.-type double blast-pipes and chimneys and A.C.F.I. feed water pumps and heaters. The superheat temperature was raised to 380°C. A further series of rebuilds of earlier classes, 231.B. and 231.E., became 231.H. and had a B.P. of 284 lb/sq in.

78. Four-cylinder compound 4—6—2 No. 231.F.413 ex P-O. This was one of 386 four-cylinder de Glehn compounds built for the Travaux Publics between 1914 and 1923, which went to the Etat, the Est and the P-O and one to the Nord. All were rebuilt in various ways between 1933 and 1937, many with poppet valves and double blast-pipes. Series 231.F., however, retained much of the appearance of the original engines.

79. Four-cylinder compound 4—6—2 No. 231.E.3 on an express from Belgium to Paris. This was one of 20 Chapelon 1934 rebuilds of P-O Pacifics, which together with 28 new engines (1936-7) were acquired by the Nord. The L.P. cylinders were inside the frames and 4 sets of Walschaert gear operated Dabeg O.C. valves.

80. Four cylinder de Glehn—du Bousquet compound 4—6—2 No. 231.C.88. The final (1931) development of the Nord Super Pacific. They required expert handling and could be driven as simples, semi-compounds or compounds.

43

81. Three-cylinder 4—6—4 No. 232.R.3 on a Lille-Paris express. Eight stoker-fired 4—6—4s designed for the Nord by de Caso came into service after the formation of the S.N.C.F., the first seven (three three-cylinder simples series 232.R. and four four-cylinder compounds series 232.S.) in 1940-41. All had identical boilers, Lemaitre blast-pipes and R.C. Dabeg valves.

82. Four-cylinder compound 4—6—4 No. 232.U.1. This, the eighth of the Nord 4—6—4s, was modified by Chapelon and appeared in 1949. It had piston valves, Houlet superheater and roller bearings on all axles. The L.P. cylinders were outside. All eight 4—6—4s worked between Paris and Lille and Paris and Aulnoye.

44

83. Four-cylinder compound 4—8—2 No. 241.P.27 on Brest-Paris express leaving St. Brieuc. Both the inside H.P. cylinders and the outside L.P. had piston valves and the cut-off was not independent. The 241.P. had mechanical stokers, Houlet superheaters and Kylchap blast-pipes. Most were built for the P.L.M. main line, but seven went to the Nord. Displaced from these routes by electrification, many ended their days on the Le Mans-Brest main line.

84. Four-cylinder compound 4—8—2 No. 241.A.50. The first 4—8—2 in Europe was built for the C. de F. de l'Est in 1925. After trials, a further 40 were built for the Est in 1929-31. These were followed by 49 for the Etat, of which No. 241.A.50 was one. However, this company did not like them and they were sold to the Est. They were all hand-fired de Glehn—du Bousquet compounds with Belpaire boilers. Although excellent machines, they were heavy on the track and their speed was limited to 110 Km/hr (69 m.p.h.).

85. Three-cylinder compound 4—8—4 No. 242.A.1. This engine had two L.P. cylinders outside and one H.P. cylinder inside the frames. Three sets of Walschaert gear operated Willoteaux valves for the L.P. cylinders and Tricks valves for the H.P. cylinder. A Houlet superheater gave the high steam temperature of 425°C. and there were two Nicholson thermic syphons in the firebox. A triple Kylchap blast-pipe was provided and the engine was, of course, stoker-fired.

86. 2—10—2 four-cylinder compound freight locomotive No. 151.A.3, ex-P.L.M. Railway. Ten of these locomotives went into service in 1932. The H.P. cylinders drove the rear six coupled wheels and the L.P. cylinders the first four. Inside coupling rods between the second and third coupled axles, both of which were cranked, synchronised the two groups. R.C. Dabeg poppet valves were used for both the H.P. and the L.P. cylinders, the drive for each side being independent and taken from a return crank on the second driving wheel of each side. After the formation of the S.N.C.F., these engines were sent to the Est Region for use on the heavy mineral trains in the Basin of Briey, and with the electrification of these lines they became redundant and were scrapped.

Facing Page

87. (top) 2—8—2 No. 141.C.83 on a freight near St. Brieuc. 250 of these engines were built for the Etat in 1921-23 and were rebuilt in 1932-47. This was a straight-forward two-cylinder simple mixed-traffic design.

88. Oil-burning 2—8—2 No. 141.R.779 on a fast freight leaving Nîmes. American builders supplied 1,340 of these engines to the S.N.C.F. in 1945-7, but 17 were lost at sea. Rugged two-cylinder machines with bar frames, 719 were stoker-fired and 604 used fuel oil. They were prominent among the last of steam in France.

89. Ex P.L.M. four-cylinder compound 2—8—2s Nos. 141.E.651 and 141.E.477 on an express from Nîmes to Paris over the heavily graded Cevennes line. These 2—8—2s were the mixed-traffic version of the P.L.M. Pacifics, Series 141.E. being 1940-50 rebuilds of two earlier series built between 1919 and 1934. Rebuilding followed much the same pattern as that of the Pacifics. Compound Mikados were first used on the P.L.M. in 1913.

90. Four-cylinder compound 2—8—2 No. 141.P.305. This was the S.N.C.F. development of the P.L.M. 141.E. (above). 318 were built from 1942 to 1952, all with stokers and Kylchap or P.L.M. type blast-pipes. The H.P. cylinders, outside, had piston valves; the L.P., inside, had Willoteaux valves. The cut-off was in a fixed ratio and not independent.

91. 2—8—0 No. 140.C.195 of the Est Region on a freight train near Gironcourt. The Est and the Etat shared 330 of these simple engines, which were supplied through the Artilleries Lourdes Voies Ferrées (A.L.V.F.) between 1913 and 1920. Some were built by the North British Locomotive Co.

92. Four-cylinder compound 2—10—0 No. 150.P.46. Between 1939 and 1951, 110 of these engines were built for the S.N.C.F. They were a further development of the Nord 150.B. and the "family likeness" to the Nord Super Pacific is very obvious. Although built essentially for heavy coal traffic, the 2—10—0s were often used as mixed-traffic engines. They were beautifully balanced and could work 550-*tonne* passenger trains at a sustained 61 m.p.h. on 1 in 200 gradients.

93. Three-cylinder 2—10—0 No. 150.C.568 on a mineral train at Longuyon. The S.N.C.F. ultimately had 118 of these engines, which were Prussian State Railways Class G-12. They were used mostly on the Est; the Etat and the Est Series 150.E. were developed from them. A form of conjugated valve gear was used for the middle valve.

94. Three cylinder 2—10—0 No. 150.E.94 working freight near Longuyon. Between 1924 and 1930, 192 of these engines were built for the Est and 10 for the Etat. They followed closely the design of the Prussian G-12 but had slightly smaller cylinders, though the axle-load was 1 *tonne* more. ▼

▲**95.** 4—6—0 No. 230.K.405. Ex P-O, sold to
the Etat 1934-38. At St. Brieuc, Ouest Region.
A two-cylinder simple of uncomplicated
design; the "Stanier Class 5" of the P-O.

▲**96.** Oil burning four cylinder compound 4—6—0 No. 230.K.241 of the Est. These
engines, built between 1905 and 1926, were rebuilt and modified between 1932 and 1946.
In 1948 twelve were streamlined and converted to burn oil fuel in order to work light,
high-speed, pneumatic-tyred trains between Paris and Strasbourg.

97. Four-cylinder
de Glehn—du Bousquet
compound 4—6—0 No.
230.D.57, ex-Nord. These
engines were built before
the First War and were
reconstructed with piston
valve cylinders and
Lemaître blast-pipes.

98. 2—8—2 T No. 141.TA.462, ex P-O, with a weed-killing train at Angoulême. Two-cylinder engines, widely used in the mountain districts of the *Massif Central.*

99. 2—8—2 T No. 141.TC.18, ex-Nord, on a suburban push-and-pull train at Paris Nord. Built 1932-5, these fine engines had Cossart valves.

100. 2—8—2 T No. 141.TB.439 ex-Est working a suburban train through Pantin. These were the smaller of two classes of 2—8—2T used for suburban trains from the Gare de l'Est.

101. 0—10—0T No. 050.TQ.10 at Paris Nord. Built 1948-9, they were the last of many 0—10—0Ts used by the S.N.C.F. The design was a modification of similar engines built for the P-O and the Midi in 1908-14. Considerable side play was provided in the first, third and fifth axles.

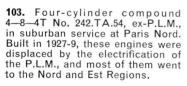

102. 2—10—2T No. 151.TQ.13. These were the S.N.C.F. version of a 1928 design for the Ceinture. Like the 050.TQ. (above), they were two-cylinder simples.

103. Four-cylinder compound 4—8—4T No. 242.TA.54, ex-P.L.M., in suburban service at Paris Nord. Built in 1927-9, these engines were displaced by the electrification of the P.L.M., and most of them went to the Nord and Est Regions.

GERMAN FEDERAL RAILWAY

Deutsche Bundesbahn: D.B.

Gauge: 4ft 8½in (1.435m)

The railways of the eight individual German States came under the unified control of the Reichsbahn in 1920. In 1924 the Reichsbahn was succeeded by the State Railway Company, but a fully state-owned and operated Deutsche Reichsbahn became effective in 1937 and included the railways of the conquered countries. After the Second War, the railways of East Germany retained the old title while those of West Germany became the Deutsche Bundesbahn.

The first steam locomotive in Germany was built by the Royal Iron Foundry, Berlin, in 1816 for the Silesian coal mines. It had two vertical cylinders and worked on the Blenkinsop rack and pinion principle with four carrying wheels.

Modern German locomotive practice dates from the introduction of new standard types by the Reichsbahn Company after 1924, and most of the designs showed the influence of the Prussian State Railway. Many locomotives of the individual State Railways, mostly, again, the Prussian State Railway, did, however, survive to the last days of steam, albeit often in countries other than Germany, whence they had gone as reparations after both Wars. Most prolific of all were the Prussian 4—6—os of Class P–8 (Plates 33 and 118) and the freight engine counterpart, the 0—8—os of Class G–8/1 (Plate 46). Although many of both types remained in Germany, it is true to say that they were to be found on all standard gauge railways of Continental Europe and the Near East at some time since 1918.

Other noteworthy late survivors of the original State Railways were the four-cylinder compound Maffei Pacifics first built in 1908 for the Bavarian State Railway, of which they were Class S–3/6. Over the years 159 were built, the last 18 by Henschel in 1930 for the Reichsbahn Company. Batches varied in dimensions, but all had bar frames, and some were rebuilt during the 1950s with larger, all-welded boilers to become D.B. Type 18/6 (Plate 104).

From the period 1922–27 interesting engines were the three-cylinder 2—8—2s of Class P–10 designed by the Prussian State Railway but built under Reichsbahn direction. Part of the drive for the inside piston valve was taken from an outside return crank. These engines lasted into the last days of steam, but with a 19-*tonne* axle-load they were not found outside Germany.

Apart from experimental types, all the Reichsbahn standard types were two-cylinder or three-cylinder simples, varying in size and axle-load according to the duties for which they were designed.

Express passenger locomotives were Pacifics, mixed-traffic locomotives were Mikados, and for heavy freight the 2—10—0 was universal. A neat 2—6—0 design was produced for branch-line work with a 2—6—2 tank engine version for suburban duties. This last type was enlarged into a 2—8—2T for heavily graded lines. Very large 2—10—2 tank engines were provided for heavy freight duties in mountainous districts and for banking. (Very similar engines to these were built for Turkey [Plate 316].) Several other types appeared including 2—6—2s, 4—6—4s, 2—10—2s and 4—6—4Ts; but they were not built in great numbers and they did not survive to the last days of steam in Western Germany; some remained, however, on the active list in Eastern Germany. Some compound locomotives were built, but apart from the Bavarian engines already noted, they were only a part of a very big programme of steam locomotive research and experiment which included turbine locomotives, the use of very high pressure steam, multi-cylinder locomotives and condensing tenders.

After the Second War, the Deutsche Bundesbahn introduced three new types of tank engines (0—10—0, 2—6—4 and 2—8—4); a series of 2—6—2 tender locomotives with which it was intended to replace the Class P–8; and two three-cylinder Pacifics, which were of the most advanced design in Europe. The most important post-war development, however, was the rebuilding of many of the former Reichsbahn standard 4—6—2s and 2—8—2s with new and larger welded boilers and with roller bearings to the big ends and in some cases to all axles. Many engines were converted to burn oil fuel. Another large-scale experiment was the fitting of two 2—10—0s with Franco-Crosti boilers (Plate 116), and 25 with Crosti boilers. These latter became a standard type (Plate 117).

The future motive power for most of the main lines of the D.B. is electric. The standard electrification is 16⅔-cycle, 15kV, single-phase A.C., with overhead conductors. Extensive use is made of diesel power on non-electrified lines, the transmissions being hydraulic. The development and extensive use of electric railcars powered by traction batteries is a unique feature of modern German motive power.

104. Four-cylinder compound 4—6—2 No. 18.608, Bavarian Class S3/6, rebuilt with a larger, all-welded boiler, leaving Ulm with a train for Friedrichshafen.

105. 4—6—2 No. 03.013 with an express for Hamburg at Flensburg. Type 03 originated in 1930 as a smaller and lighter version of Type 01 (Plate 106). Engines up to No. 03.123 had a maximum axle-load of 17 *tonnes* while for Nos.03.124 to 03.298 it was 18 *tonnes.*▼

106. 4—6—2 No. 01.052 on a Nürnberg-Munich express near Lüngenbrücke. Decorations on the deflector plates celebrate Whitsuntide. 241 of these Reichsbahn standard heavy Pacifics were built between 1925 and 1937. The axle-load was 20 *tonnes*.

107. Rebuilt 4—6—2 No. 01.180. From 1951 many standard Reichsbahn engines were rebuilt with larger, all-welded boilers and with roller bearings for big ends and in some cases for all axles. Exhaust from auxiliaries was arranged in the perimeter of the large-diameter chimney casing; the engines retained their single blast-pipes and the 01s remained hand-fired coal-burners. ▼

108. Rebuilt three-cylinder 4—6—2 No. 03.1001 with a south-bound express leaving Cologne. These "Light-weights" had an axle-load of only 18 *tonnes* when built in 1939. From 1951 many were rebuilt in the same way as Type O1 (Plate 107), though a few burned oil. The eight-wheel bogie tenders had covers for the coal bunkers.

109. Rebuilt three-cylinder 4—6—2 No. 01.1101. With the exception of the two Type 10 Pacifics, these were the most powerful express locomotives of the D.B. When introduced in 1939 their maximum axle-load was 20.3 *tonnes* and they had 10-wheel tenders. From 1951 they were rebuilt with larger welded boilers, and most as oil burners; they retained their single blast-pipes despite the wide chimney casings. T.I.A. water treatment and roller bearings helped them to put up some impressive utilisation figures, often exceeding those of the V-200 diesel-hydraulic locomotives.

110. Oil burning three-cylinder 4—6—2 No. 10.002. Two Pacifics of Type 10 were built by Krupp for the Bundesbahn in 1956. The first burned coal but had auxiliary oil firing to assist the fireman on heavy trains. It was later altered to burn only oil fuel, becoming identical with No. 10.002. Unlike the standard Reichsbahn engines, which had bar frames, the Type 10 had frames built up from I-section plate and welded. Roller bearings were used for all axles and for big and little ends. The boiler was welded and had a combustion chamber but no arch tubes or syphons. It had 44 large superheater tubes and a superheat temperature of 450°C was attained, but owing to the tendency for oil-burning engines to burn superheater elements, arrangements were made for water to be admitted to the header should this temperature be exceeded. The outside cylinders drove the second coupled axle, the inside cylinder the first, and three sets of Walschaert gear were provided, reversing being air-assisted. Both engines had double blast-pipes and chimneys. One of the many refinements was the fitting in the spectacles of electrically driven rotating glass screens of the "clear vision" type. These Pacifics represented the furthest development of the European steam locomotive.

111. View showing the balanced lids fitted to tender coal space to prevent coal dust being swept on to the foot-plate by back draught through the bunker.

112. 2—8—2 No. 41.255 on a train for Hannover leaving Göttingen. 366 of these mixed-traffic engines were built for the Reichsbahn between 1936 and 1941. There were two types, the difference being in the weight distribution. Although the total engine weight was the same, one type had a maximum axle-load of 17.6 *tonnes* the other type 19.7 *tonnes*.

113. Rebuilt 2—8—2 No. 41.166. The Bundesbahn rebuilt a number of these engines with larger welded boilers, and in some cases new cylinders and roller-bearing big and little ends. They remained hand-fired coal burners and had bunker-lids.

▲114. Three-cylinder 2—10—0 No. 44.1440 with a south-bound freight train near Bebra. Type 44 was introduced in 1925 and became the standard heavy freight engine of the Reichsbahn and the Bundesbahn. Construction ceased in 1949 after more than 2,000 had been built, many, with detail differences, in France, Austria and Denmark during and after the Second War. Some engines had mechanical stokers but despite 49 sq ft of grate area most were hand-fired. The German Railways never adopted mechanical stokers on a big scale.

115. 2—10—0 No. 50.929. In 1927 Type 43, a two-cylinder 2—10—0 with 20-*tonnes* axle-load, was introduced on the Reichsbahn. It was followed in 1938 by Type 50 with an axle-load of only 15.5 *tonnes,* which became the basic design for 10,650 locomotives built in Germany and elsewhere until 1949. Type 52, the *Kriegslokomotiven* (Plate 312), were lighter, with a 15-*tonne* ax!e-load and, in some cases, plate frames. Nearly 8,000 were built between 1942 and 1950. Heavier engines with 17-*tonnes* axle-load were Type 42 (Plate 9) of which 900 were built. Type 50 remained the standard freight engine of the D.B. until the end of steam and, with Type 44, long outlasted the other 2—10—0s in Germany. Both these types had a maximum speed of 50 m.p.h. and were often used in passenger service.

116. 2—10—0 No. 42.9001 fitted with Franco-Crosti boiler with two economisers. Two engines only were so equipped and were scrapped in 1959 as the locomotives themselves were of a, by then, non-standard Bundesbahn type, and the single-economiser Crosti boiler was found more reliable. (See Pages 54, 100 and 103.)

117. 2—10—0 No. 50.4019 with Crosti boiler. Severe corrosion of economiser tubes, chimney elbows, etc., was caused by the formation of sulphuric acid in the cooled and retarded flue gases. The trouble was largely overcome by the use of chrome steel in the worst affected parts, and the 25 Crosti engines became a standard class. (See Pages 76, 105 and 134.)

118. 4—6—0 No. 38.1639, Prussian Class P-8 (see also Plate 33) on a train for Mühldorf at Munich. Some 3,850 of these excellent mixed-traffic engines were built between 1906 and 1924 and were used in many European and Near East countries. The boilers and many details were interchangeable with those of the 0—8—0s of Class G-8/1 (Plate 46). In their last days on the Bundesbahn many were fitted with small standard deflector plates and had semi-elliptical tenders from scrapped *Kriegslokomotiven*. They were used for a wide variety of duties, including the working of push-and-pull suburban trains. In 1951 two P-8s were converted to 4—6—4 tank locomotives by replacing the tender with a tank and bunker riding on a four-wheel bogie.

119. 2—6—2 No. 23.053 with roller bearings, on a train for Frankfurt, at Rudesheim. 105 Type 23 were built between 1950 and 1959, the last steam locomotives for the D.B. Intended as replacements of the P-8s, but the rapid advance of diesel and electric traction upset this programme. Earlier engines of Type 23 had plain bearings, but all had wide chimney casings which accommodated pump exhausts. The axle-load was 17 *tonnes* but, as in Type 41, by altering the weight distribution a maximum axle-load of 19 *tonnes* could be obtained for service with heavy trains on suitable track. The all-welded boilers had channel type foundation rings; the frames were of steel plate welded up as a single unit. ▼

▲**120.** Lightweight 2—6—0 No. 24.041 with a train for Büchen leaving Lübeck. Built between 1927 and 1938, a total of 115 of these useful little engines were in service. The last 20 had Krauss-Helmholtz leading trucks.

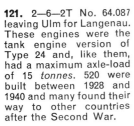

121. 2—6—2T No. 64.087 leaving Ulm for Langenau. These engines were the tank engine version of Type 24 and, like them, had a maximum axle-load of 15 *tonnes*. 520 were built between 1928 and 1940 and many found their way to other countries after the Second War.

122. 2—8—2T No. 93.712, Prussian Class T-14/1. These engines were introduced in 1919 and with an axle-load of 17.3 *tonnes* they were a heavier version of the Prussian Class T-14 of 1914. Many were built and they were widely used for freight and suburban passenger duties in Germany and many countries of Western Europe.

123. 2—6—0T No. 74.637 at Hamburg (Altona). A very large number of Prussian State Railway Class T-12 were built between 1902 and 1921 and many went to other countries as reparations.

124. 2—8—2T No. 86.070 on a Dirringhausen train at Olpe. One of a large class of Reichsbahn tank engines built 1928-1943. Many of the later engines had Krauss-Helmholtz leading and trailing trucks.

125. 0—10—0T No. 82.016. One of the heavy shunting engines (18-*tonne* axle) introduced by the Bundesbahn in 1950.

126. 2—6—4T No. 66.002 was one of two light suburban tank engines (15-*tonne* axle) built in 1955. As diesel and electric traction was by then becoming well established, no further engines of the type were built.

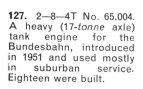

127. 2—8—4T No. 65.004. A heavy (17-*tonne* axle) tank engine for the Bundesbahn, introduced in 1951 and used mostly in suburban service. Eighteen were built.

BRITISH RAILWAYS: B.R.

Gauge : 4ft 8½in (1.435m)

On 1st January, 1948, the inland transport (excluding air transport) and the docks and harbours of Great Britain were nationalised but not co-ordinated, and the British Transport Commission (B.T.C.) was constituted. British Railways became part of the B.T.C., bringing under public ownership four large companies which, in their turn, had amalgamated some 25 major companies in 1923.

The first steam locomotive to run in Britain and in the world was an 0—4—0 with a single vertical cylinder, built by Richard Trevithick at Pen-y-darren for the iron works at that place. It made its first run on 13th February, 1804.

The British people always endowed their steam locomotives with human attributes, and bestowed names on many of them from the earliest times. This extraordinary love of man for machine was undoubtedly encouraged by the beauty of design and excellence of workmanship and finish for which British steam locomotives were famous. Unfortunately many of these elegant machines were shockingly inefficient and badly designed from the point of view of accessibility and maintenance. There was often no standardisation of parts between different classes, and not until the late 1920s was it generally appreciated that one good design could carry out many diverse duties for which special classes had previously been demanded.

Britain was always a "small engine" country and only after the First War, and more particularly after the amalgamation of 1923, from when modern British steam power dates, was any serious progress made towards a bigger engine policy. Such a policy was always at a disadvantage on account of stringent loading gauge restrictions, and for this reason also, three- and four-cylinder locomotives were commonplace in Britain, while after 1923 compounding was, with the exception of a few experimental engines, limited to one series of excellent 4—4—0s originally built by the Midland Railway and developed by the L.M. & S.R. Articulated locomotives were confined to one series of Garratts for the L.M. & S., and a single large banking engine for the L. & N.E.

Another peculiarity of British practice was that all the companies had their own works and constructed most of their own steam locomotives, a state of affairs unique in Western Europe and indeed in most of the world.

There were many famous C.M.E.s in British Railway history; before 1923 the greatest of them all was J. G. Churchward of the Great Western, who had, at that time, a unique appreciation of the economics of the steam locomotive, and his engines were unequalled for performance and economy anywhere else in the Kingdom, if not in the world. Ultimately his influence was felt by all other railways, though not until the late 1920s were his principles universally embodied in new designs.

In 1931 a Churchward pupil, W. A. Stanier, became C.M.E. of the L.M. & S.R., and in his designs he adopted many G.W. principles, improving on them in the light of more recent practice. He introduced a high degree of standardisation, and some of his designs formed the basis of those for British Railways 17 years later.

On the L. & N.E.R., Nigel Gresley was another great engineer, much of his greatness, like that of Churchward, stemming from his willingness to learn from others. However, only after he had adopted the G.W. principles of steam distribution did his designs become outstandingly successful and economical.

Gresley's one-time assistant, O. V. S. Bulleid, became C.M.E. of the Southern in 1938 and was the most advanced-thinking locomotive engineer of his day. As with Chapelon in France, however, the Second War and afterwards nationalisation and the increasing use of other forms of motive power prevented the further development of his most interesting designs.

After nationalisation extensive trials resulted in the evolution of 11 standard classes, which with some existing classes, covered the country's locomotive requirements. With the exception of the Class 9 2—10—0s all the classes were six-coupled with two simple cylinders. A single three-cylinder 4—6—2 of Class 8 appeared in 1954, but no further engines of this class were built. The standard engines were straightforward machines designed for economy of running and maintenance, and few major modifications have been made to them.

The future motive power of British Railways is as diverse as were the steam engines of the original companies. Systems of electrification of various main and suburban lines are 660/750V D.C., third rail; 1,500V D.C., overhead conduction; and monophase 50-cycle A.C., at 25kV and 6.25kV. Diesel traction is widely used and there is a heterogeneous collection of locomotives of many types and little standardisation. Electric, hydraulic and mechanical transmissions are used. Diesel railcars, train sets and railbuses of more than a hundred different types are used for secondary and suburban services. Some diesel-electric m.-u. Pullman sets provide a few fast and luxurious inter-city services, comparable with those of the T.E.E. trains.

66

128. Three-cylinder 4—4—0 No. 30923 *Bradfield* on a Victoria—Dover express. The Southern Class V locomotives (the "Schools" class) were introduced in 1930 when other countries had long since ceased to use 4—4—0s on main-line duties. The "Schools" were built for the Eastern Section—especially the Hastings line—where weight and loading gauge restrictions prevented the use of large locomotives. They had three cylinders with independent valve gear, maximum axle-load was 21 tons, and with a tractive effort of 25,135 lb they were the most powerful European 4—4—0s. Forty were built of which twenty were later fitted with multiple jet blast-pipes. They were superb machines, popular with both footplate men and shed staff.

129. Ex-L.M.S. 4—4—0 No. 40563 piloting three-cylinder 4—6—2 No. 34041 *Wilton* (Southern unrebuilt "West Country" class) on an express from Liverpool on the S. & D. J. line.

The inside-cylinder 4—4—0 was a favourite design on most British Railways, especially the Midland, whose superheater rebuilds of older engines formed the basis for this L.M.S. design of 1928. These very economical engines were among late survivors of steam in Britain.

130. Ex-L.N.E.R. three-cylinder 2—6—0 No. 61964 Class K-3/2 with a train from Lincoln to Sheffield. In 1918 the first Gresley three-cylinder 2—6—0 with a 6 ft diameter boiler was introduced and this became L.N.E. Class K-3 in 1923. Nearly 200 were built and the design included the standard Gresley derived valve motion for the inside cylinders, a feature used in all subsequent three-cylinder engines for the L.N.E.R. during Gresley's life. The original three-cylinder 2—6—0s were the "guinea-pig" engines for the Great Northern Pacifics which appeared in 1922.

131. B.R. standard 2—6—0 No. 76010 Class 4. This picture gives a good idea of the excellent accessibility of working parts. There were three series of standard 2—6—0s of Classes 2, 3 and 4 respectively, the Class 2 being the lightest. They were all mixed-traffic engines and Classes 2 and 3 had 2—6—2 tank engine versions. Also in Class 4 were standard 4—6—0s and 2—6—4Ts (Plate 152).

▲132. Ex-G.W. 4—6—0 No. 7902 *Eaton Mascot Hall*. The two-cylinder 4—6—0s of the Great Western were first built by Churchward in 1905 and the type was developed until it reached its final form with the "Counties" in 1945. By far the most prolific were the "Halls", of which 330 were built and which were a mixed-traffic version of the earlier "Saints". The last 71, of which No. 7902 was one, were introduced in 1944 and had various modifications including larger superheaters. All the G.W. two-cylinder 4—6—0s had cylinders with the long piston stroke of 30in.

133. B.R. Standard 4—6—0 No. 73087 Class 5 at work on the Kent Coast line of the Southern Region. Modern mixed-traffic 4—6—0s were in service with all four companies before nationalisation. The standard engines had roller bearings to all axles and modern practice was followed in all details, resulting in a free running and economical design. They were developed from the famous Stanier Class 5 of the L.M.S. which, with 842 engines formed one of the largest British classes (Plate 149). ▼

134. Ex-G.W.R. four-cylinder 4—6—0 No. 6025 *King Henry III* on an up express taking water at Aynho troughs. The 30 "Kings" introduced in 1927 were, at that time, the most powerful British express locomotives, with a tractive effort of 40,285 lb. The axle-load was $22\frac{1}{2}$ tons. From 1947 they were given larger superheaters and from 1955 double blast-pipes and chimneys. The "Kings" represented the final development of the G.W. four-cylinder 4—6—0 although engines of the earlier and smaller "Castle" class were built until 1950.

135. Ex-L.M.S. three-cylinder 4—6—0 No. 46152 *The King's Dragoon Guardsman* on the down "Red Rose" Express climbing Camden Bank. The "Royal Scots", introduced in 1927, were the first big L.M.S. passenger engines. From 1943 all were rebuilt with new cylinders having improved steam distribution, taper boilers and double blast-pipes. Classed 7P, with an axle load of nearly $20\frac{1}{2}$ tons and a tractive effort of 33,150 lb, they were one of the most successful modern express locomotives. ▼

136. Ex-L.M.S. four-cylinder 4—6—2 No. 46244 *King George VI,* "Coronation" class, with a down express. W. A. Stanier's first Pacifics for the L.M.S. ("Princess" class) were introduced in 1933 and the streamlined "Coronations" in 1937. These latter engines had larger boilers than the "Princesses" and two sets of Walschaert valve gear, the inside valves being driven through rocking shafts. Twelve were built without streamlining and all the others had it removed from 1946. They were fine, rugged machines which steamed well and rode superbly. Classed 8P, their tractive effort was 40,000 lb and their maximum axle-load 22½ tons. The last two were built by Ivatt in 1947 and had roller bearings to all axles.

137. Ex-Southern three-cylinder 4—6—2 No. 34013 *Okehampton,* rebuilt "West Country" class. O. V. Bulleid's "Merchant Navy" class Pacifics appeared in 1941 and the lighter "West Countries" four years later. As built (Plate 129) both classes were "air-smoothed" and had multiple jet blast-pipes and Bulleid radial valve-gear which was chain driven and, with middle crosshead, connecting rod and crank, pump-lubricated in an oil bath. Other features new to British practice were welded steel fireboxes with two thermic syphons, steam-operated firehole doors, cast-steel wheel centres and electric lighting. Both classes suffered from instability of valve events mainly due to chain wear, and obstruction of the enginemen's view ahead by drifting exhaust steam and smoke. From 1956 all "Merchant Navies" and most "West Countries" were rebuilt with three sets of Walschaert gear and the air smoothing was removed. Boiler pressure was reduced from 280 to 250 lb/sq in. Other features were retained and both classes became outstandingly successful. ▼

138. Ex-L.N.E.R. three-cylinder 4—6—2 No. 60017 Class A4 *Silver Fox* passing Harringay with a down express. The first Gresley Pacifics were built in 1922 for the Great Northern, and the A4s were their direct descendants. They had Gresley's standard derived valve motion for the middle valve which, unless well maintained, allowed over-running of the valve with consequent heating of the middle big-end. Late in their lives, re-design of this big-end, the replacement of nickel-chrome steel rods by those of normal steel and the fitting of double blast-pipes made the A4s fully able to cope with the reduced maintenance, poor coal and often indifferent handling of the last days of steam. No. 60022 holds the world record for steam, 126 m.p.h., and the A4s will long be remembered for all that was best in steam motive power.

139. Three-cylinder 4—6—2 No. 60141 Class A1 *Abbotsford* on the up "Yorkshire Pullman". The fifty A1s were the last East Coast Pacifics; designed for the L.N.E., they went into service after nationalisation. They had three sets of Walschaert gear and double blast-pipes. They were more powerful than any of the Gresley Pacifics but were very light on maintenance. ▼

140. Three-cylinder 4—6—2 Class 8 No. 71000 *Duke of Gloucester*. This was the final British Railways steam locomotive design, a great engine which may be compared with No. 242A.1 of the S.N.C.F. and Type 10 of the D.B. Owing to the adoption of other forms of motive power, it remained the solitary example of its class, and as its driving and firing were quite different from the L.M.S. "Coronation" class (Plate 136) with which it worked, it was seldom handled correctly and its performance suffered. No. 71000 had British Caprotti valves, which gave superb cylinder performance and economy of steam consumption and maintenance. The boiler was identical with that of Class 7 (Plate 141) except that the firebox was 1 ft longer, giving a larger grate. A double blast-pipe and chimney were fitted. All axles of both engine and tender had roller bearings.

141. 4—6—2 Class 7 No. 70037 *Hereward the Wake*. There were two standard two-cylinder Pacific designs, the "Britannia" (Class 7) and the lighter "Clan" (Class 6). The former were excellent machines which steamed well and had a good front end. Roller bearings were fitted to all axles. They had single blast-pipes and were, of course, hand-fired. Their best work was done on the Eastern Region and they completely transformed the London—Norwich services. The "Clans" were never so successful.

73

142. Ex-L.N.E. three-cylinder 2—6—2 No. 60963 Class V2 with double blast-pipe and chimney. These engines first appeared in 1936 and were intended for fast freight service. The first engine of the class was named *Green Arrow*, which was also the name given to a special freight service with guaranteed delivery time. 184 were built, and they were able to work the fastest express trains as well as freight, being true mixed-traffic engines. Gresley's standard derived valve motion for the inside valve followed the same layout as for the Pacifics, while the boiler was a shorter version of that for the A3, with a banjo-dome housing a slotted steam collector. In their later days many had new cylinders with outside steam-pipes while several were fitted with double blast-pipes. This modification greatly improved their steaming.

143. Ex-G.W. 2—8—0 No. 2825 with a northbound freight train near Craven Arms. These G.W. engines were the first British 2—8—0s and 167 were built between their introduction, in 1903, and 1942. They had coned boilers with top feed, and although later batches varied in detail, basically the design remained unchanged over nearly 40 years. Superheaters were fitted to the class from 1909 onwards.

144. Ex-L.N.E. 2—8—0 No. 63842 Class O-4/3 on an ore train near Darnall. This was J. G. Robinson's 1911 design for the Great Central, who built 273. Many others (including No. 63842) were built for the R.O.D. during the First War and served overseas. In 1919 the G.W.R. bought 50 and in 1924 the L.N.E.R. 125 of the R.O.D. engines. During the Second War, 92 from the L.N.E.R. were taken over by the Government and sent to the Middle East. Over the years, many engines of the original design have been altered in various ways and in 1944, 58 were completely rebuilt with new cylinders, Walschaert valve gear and a standard round-top boiler, to become Class O-1.

145. Ex-L.M.S. 2—8—0 No. 48109 on an up coal train near St. Albans. This was Stanier's 1935 design for the L.M.S. and was said to have been based on the G.W. 28XX class. They were excellent and very popular engines and many were built for the War Department during the Second War and served overseas. Later in the War, the design was simplified and given a parallel boiler, to become the W.D. Austerity 2—8—0, of which 935 were built (Plate 175).

146. British Railways standard 2—10—0 No. 92039 Class 9. Except for one experimental tank engine built for the Great Eastern Railway in 1902 and an 0—10—0 banking engine built for the Midland Railway in 1920, no ten-coupled engines ran in Britain until 1944 when the War Department Austerity 2—10—0s appeared, 25 of which were ultimately taken into British Railways stock. In 1954 the B.R. Standard Class 9 was introduced and 251 were built, including the last steam locomotive built for British Railways, No. 92220 *Evening Star*. The Class 9 proved itself to be a most successful and versatile locomotive, capable of very high speeds in express train service, 90 m.p.h. having been recorded on one occasion. The maximum axle load was 15½ tons and the middle pair of coupled wheels were without flanges. Ten engines were built with Crosti boilers but the economisers were later removed and the smaller boilers retained. **Plate 147** (below) shows No. 92021 in this condition. Other major modifications were the fitting of double blast-pipes and chimneys to many of the class, and a Giesl ejector to one engine. Three engines ran for a time with Berkley mechanical stokers, but these were later removed. The last engine, *Evening Star*, had a copper-topped double chimney and was painted and lined out in British Railways livery.

148. Ex-L.M.S. (Midland) 0—6—0 No. 43808 with an up parcels train at Elstree. Inside-cylinder, non-superheater 0—6—0s were built in hundreds for most British railways about the turn of the century and many remained until the last days of steam.

149. Ex-L.M.S. (Caledonian superheater 0—6—0 No. 57667) piloting a Stanier class 5 4—6—0 on a freight at Luib. The superheated 0—6—0 was another popular British type which was built in large numbers from about 1910 until 1942. Appearance and design varied greatly according to the ideas of the parent company.

150. Ex-Southern superheater 0—6—0 Class Q1 No. 33015 was one of O. V. S. Bulleid's Austerity engines built during the Second War, in 1942, at a time when ferrous and other metals were very scarce. They were the last British 0—6—0s and had multiple-jet blast-pipes and cast-steel wheel centres. Despite their unconventional appearance they were excellent machines.

F

151. Ex-G.W. 2—6—2T No. 4147 on a Worcester—Oxford slow train. The G.W. introduced the 2—6—2T with 5ft 8in wheels in 1903 and large numbers were subsequently built, the last in 1949 after nationalisation. They were highly competent machines which were used all over the system for local and suburban duties. There were detail modifications and improvements in later batches, and a number of the earlier engines were rebuilt. A large number of smaller 2—6—2T with 4ft 7½in wheels were built by the G.W. for branch-line work.

152. B.R. standard class 4 2—6—4T No. 80145 on a London (Victoria)—Tunbridge Wells train. These engines were the tank engine version of the standard class 4 4—6—0, though, unlike these latter engines, none had double blast-pipes. They were excellent machines closely comparable with similar engines built in large numbers for the L.M.S. Like most modern locomotives in Britain, they had self-cleaning smokeboxes.

153. Ex-G.W.R. 0—6—0PT No. 7753. Inside-cylinder 0—6—0 tank engines did most of the shunting on British railways. With some 2,372 built over a period of 96 years, the most numerous were those of the G.W.R., the more recent of which had pannier tanks. With 863 examples built between 1929 and 1956, they formed the largest group of engines in Britain, and in addition to shunting were used for branch-line and push-and-pull duties, some being built with larger wheels for such work.

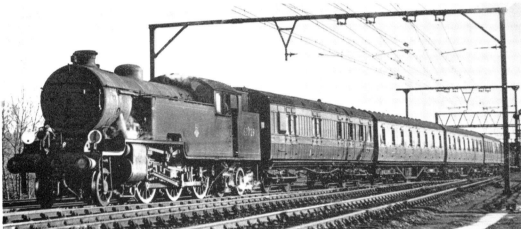

154. Ex-L.N.E. 2—6—4T Class L1 No. 67729 on a Liverpool Street—Southend train. These were the last suburban tank engines for the L.N.E.R. and were designed by Edward Thompson in 1945. The tractive effort was 32,080 lb—nearly as high as that of the Class A3 Pacific.

155. Ex-Southern three-cylinder 0—8—0T Class Z No. 953. Another powerful tank engine with a tractive effort of 29,375 lb, designed in 1929 by R. E. L. Maunsell for heavy shunting, especially on humps.

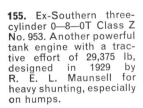

HELLENIC STATE RAILWAYS
Chemins de Fer de L'Etat Hellenique: C.E.H.

Gauges : 4ft 8½in (1.435m)
3ft 3⅜in (1.0m)

The first railway in Greece was completed between Athens and the port of Piraeus in 1869. This 10 km.-long railway was electrified in 1904 and extensions to the original line have been built. The first locomotive is unknown.

The railways in Greece were completely isolated from those of the rest of Europe until 1916.

The Hellenic State Railways came into being in 1920 and amalgamated the three major companies. Several metre-gauge systems were also ultimately taken over, including the most important and very up-to-date Piraeus-Athens-Peloponnesus Railway (S.P.A.P.).

Standard gauge steam locomotives in Greece numbered less than 200 and the most important types were all ten-couplers, being with one exception of German, Belgian, Austrian or American origin. The exception was the Class Mα consisting of twenty 2—10—2 engines built in Italy to C.E.H. designs from 1953–55. The largest class were the 0—10—0s of Class Kβ, of which 60 were built in Austria.

Modern American-built engines started with 20 2—8—2s delivered by Alco in 1916. These were two-cylinder simples with bar frames and 5ft 0in driving wheels. The next American locomotives came to Greece after the Second War and consisted of United States Army 2—8—0s (Plate 160), eight 2—10—0s built by Baldwin in 1947 (Plate 158), and several of the U.S. Army type 0—6—0T (Plate 156) of which some were in service in Britain (Southampton Docks) as well as in many other European Countries.

The locomotives of the C.E.H. were without any major national design characteristics, and each class showed plainly the country of its origin. All locomotives were two-cylinder simples and many burned oil fuel.

The future motive power of the C.E.H. is in diesel-electric and diesel-hydraulic locomotives, and diesel-hydraulic and diesel-mechanical railcars. No further electrification is envisaged.

156. 0—6—0T Class Δα No. 62 shunting at Athens. A standard Wartime U.S. Army locomotive.

157. Oil-burning 2—10—2 Class Mα No. 1017. This was one of the largest and most powerful non-articulated engines ever built for the standard-gauge railways of Western Europe (though the broad-gauge 2—10—2s of the R.E.N.F.E. (Plate 278) exceeded them in weight and power). Twenty such engines were built in Italy from 1953 to 1955, and ten were hand-fired coal-burners. The very large boiler (6ft 10in maximum inside diameter) had a welded steel firebox with four arch tubes and a grate area of 60.3sq ft, which must have made hand-firing a pretty tough job. A Kylchap double blast-pipe and chimney was fitted to all the engines.

These locomotives had welded plate frames and the leading coupled wheels, which were flangeless, formed a Krauss truck with the leading radial wheels.

The main line between Athens and Salonika, over which these engines worked, is in parts very mountainous, with a ruling gradient of 1 in 50 (2 per cent). The Second War left the track in a very poor state and much time and money was needed to bring all main lines up to first class standard. As a result of stresses set up by these factors and by certain design features, these engines gave much trouble with fractured boiler throat plates, and in 1958 were all withdrawn for reconstruction with modified boiler support and for repairs to the boilers themselves. This work was carried out by Henschel and the engines all returned to service. During their absence, the C.E.H. borrowed a number of Austrian 2—10—0s of Type 258.

158. Oil-burning 2—10—0 Class Λγ No. 991—one of eight loco-motives obtained from Baldwin as hand-fired coal burners in 1947. All had American chime whistles. The strong family resemblance to the S.N.C.F. American-built locomotives of Series 141.R. will be noted.

159. SKODA-built Oil-burning 2—10—0 Class Λα No. 909 with an express train from Salonika at Athens. These engines were similar to the Austrian Type 258, originally a Südbahn design (Plate 8), but the Greek engines have slightly larger coupled wheels, and the boilers had greater heating surface. They were also 4 *tonnes* heavier.

▲160. Oil-burning 2—8—0 Class Θγ No. 528 working a freight train between Athens and Piraeus. This was one of the U.S. Army locomotives, of which many were used in Britain, which ultimately worked on most of the standard gauge railways in Europe and North Africa. They had bar frames, and those which did not burn oil were hand fired.

161. 0—10—0 Class Kβ No. 817. Sixty engines were built by STEG of Vienna in 1922-6 to the designs of the Austrian Südbahn Type 80. Class Kα consisted of two engines built in 1912 and obtained from the Bulgarian State Railways after the First War.

162. 0—10—0 Class Kγ No. 865. Twenty were built in 1929 by Tubize and St. Léonard. They were different in appearance and details from Class Kβ but were basically the same.

Piraeus—Athens—Peloponnesus Railway, S.P.A.P.

Gauge: 3ft 3⅜in (1.0m)

The Piraeus-Athens-Peloponnesus Railway (S.P.A.P.) serves the Peloponnese peninsular, making a complete circle of this historic land from Corinth and back to Corinth. The main line to Athens crosses the Corinth Canal and then runs along the South Coast of the mainland to reach the capital. It has always been an up-to-date and well run railway and the steam locomotive stock was of great interest. Two classes of 2—8—0s and two classes of 2—8—2s were the mainstay of the line during the last days of steam and worked all the main line trains, both passenger and freight. Two classes of 2—6—0T dealt with a great variety of duties, working both local passenger and freight trains and doing all the shunting. Other engines which ran on the line were several 2—4—0Ts with superheater boilers built by Henschel in 1912 and two 0—4—4—0 four-cylinder compound Mallet tank engines built by Krauss in 1908.

The future of the S.P.A.P. is with diesel traction. Railcars, mostly by Fiat, deal with all except the heaviest passenger traffic, and diesel locomotives will do the rest of the work.

163. 2—8—0 Class E No. 728 with a freight train from Kalamé to Athens entering Megara. This was a coal-burner, one of a class built by Henschel in 1936, some of which burned oil.

164. 2—6—0T Class Z No. 507 working freight from the Piraeus to Athens. This was a non-superheater engine with slide valves and outside Allen link motion. It was built by St. Léonard in 1891 and was identical with five engines built by the same firm for the Economic Railways of Asturias.

165. 2—6—0T Class Z No. 532, one of the more numerous 2—6—0Ts with piston valves, Walschaert gear and a superheater boiler. These engines were built in 1911 by Krauss and were used on all sorts of work, from banking heavy trains on the numerous long and steep gradients, to yard shunting.

▲166. Oil-burning 2—8—2 Class △ No. 117. These fine engines were built by Breda in 1952. They were free-running machines which steamed well and rode superbly. Their maximum speed was 60km/hr. (37½ m.p.h.) and they could negotiate a curve of 80 m. radius. They were fitted with tender cabs to work heavy passenger trains tender first if required.

167. Oil-burning 2—8—2 Class △ No. 103 leaving Athens with an express for Kalamé. These typical American bar-framed engines were built by Vulcan, Wilkes-Barre in 1947. Notice the centre buffer with the coupling below it—standard practice on the S.P.A.P.

NETHERLANDS RAILWAYS COMPANY
N.V. Nederlandsche Spoorwegen: N.S.
Gauge : 4ft 8½in (1.435m)

The large number of private companies which developed the railways in Holland gradually amalgamated until two large companies, the Holland Railway Company and the Netherlands State Railway, remained. From 1920 to 1937 these companies were controlled by the state and took the title Netherlands Railways (Nederlandsche Spoorwegen). On 1st January, 1938, the state-owned Netherlands Railway Company was formed and took over complete control and ownership of all standard-gauge railways in Holland.

The first steam locomotive in Holland was a 2—2—2 with inside cylinders named *De Arend* and built by Longridge and Co. of Newcastle as their No. 119 of 1839. This locomotive, together with *Snelheid* of the same type, was built for a gauge of 6ft 4⅜in and operated on the Amsterdam-Haarlem line from 24th September, 1839. This line became part of the Holland Railway, which remained broad gauge until 1866.

Steam locomotive development in Holland came to an end in 1930 as it was decided to proceed with electrification for future motive power. This programme was completely upset by German aggression and occupation and before being driven out of Holland the Germans virtually destroyed the railways, tearing up track, blowing bridges, demolishing stations, etc. All the overhead electric equipment was torn down and 400 steam locomotives were rendered useless. This wanton destruction, however, had ultimately some advantages for it enabled the Dutch to build a new system on the most modern concepts. In the immediate post-War period, however, steam locomotives of existing types were obtained from Germany, Switzerland and France. From Britain came 103 War Department 2—10—0s 237 2—8—0s (Plate 175) and 27 0—6—0STs, while Sweden provided 35 three-cylinder 0—8—0s (Plate 176) and 15 three-cylinder 4—6—0s (Plate 177) built to orders placed in 1942 with Nydquist & Holm by the exiled Dutch Government in London. All these locomotives were, from the first, regarded only as stop-gaps until electric and diesel traction could take over, and a maximum life of 10 years was envisaged for them. Many of them were scrapped in well under this period, and the last steam locomotive in Holland was withdrawn in 1958.

The steam locomotives of the N.S. were, before the Second War, elegant machines in which beauty of design was matched by immaculate appearance, with apple green paint, copper-topped chimneys and polished brass domes and safety valve covers (where fitted). There were no very outstanding designs and apart from eight Maffei four-cylinder compound 4—6—0s built in 1916 for the Netherlands Central Railway, all engines were either two- or four-cylinder simples. Inherited from the old companies were 2—8—2Ts and 0—10—0Ts as well as a large number of smaller engines of both tender and tank varieties. Having no serious gradients in any part of the country, heavy and powerful locomotives were needed only for some coal traffic.

In the classification of N.S. locomotives P=passenger, G=goods, R=shunting, L=branch line, T=tank and O=superheated. So Class PTO/2 was a superheater passenger tank engine of Series 2.

The present and future motive power in Holland is electric, 1,500 volts D.C., with overhead conductors. On non-electrified lines diesel trainsets and locomotives are used, the transmissions being mostly electric.

168. Four-cylinder 4—6—0 No. 3701 on a northbound coal train near Nijmegen. A 1956 picture which shows the engine in post-War condition and with a tender from a W.D. 2—8—0.

169. Four-cylinder 4—6—0 No. 3776 Class PO/3. These were the best N.S. express engines and 120 were built, first by Beyer Peacock in 1910 for the Netherlands State Railway and subsequently in Holland and Germany until 1928. The last five had eight-wheeled tenders and larger cylinders and in 1936, six were streamlined. The cylinders were in line and drove the leading coupled axle and two sets of inside Walschaert gear drove the inside valves and, through rocking shafts, the outside valves. All had Belpaire boilers.

170. Four-cylinder 4—6—0 No. 3928 Class PO/4 in post-War condition. Thirty-two were built by Henschel in 1929-30. They had bar frames and larger boilers and grates than the preceding class, but the layout and drive were identical. They were heavy on coal but this may partly have been due to the preference of Dutch enginemen to drive "on the regulator". The boilers, cylinders and other parts were interchangeable with those of the 4—8—4T Class GTO/3. (Plate 183.)

171. Superheater 4—4—0 No. 1718 Class PO/1 on an express for Munich leaving Rotterdam D.P. These lovely engines were introduced on the Netherlands State Railway in 1899 and 137 were built, the majority by Beyer Peacock & Co. They had inside Stephenson link motion. After 1914 many were superheated, being provided with larger piston-valve cylinders and inside Walschaert valve gear. Some were also given new boilers with a higher working pressure. Swing-link bogies were first fitted, but gave much trouble and were replaced with bogies of the cross-slide type having laminated control springs.

172. 4—4—0 No. 1912 Class PO/1 at Rotterdam (Maas). Forty were built by Werkspoor for the Holland Railway Company between 1907 and 1913, being the Company's first superheated engines. They had piston valves above the cylinders, driven through rocking shafts by Stephenson gear, and Schmidt superheaters were fitted. They were economical and free-running engines.

173. 4—4—0 No. 2115 Class PO/2 with an express from Marseilles at Rotterdam D.P. Thirty-five of these powerful engines were built in Holland and Germany for the Holland Railway Company between 1914 and 1920. They were excellent engines and were the culmination of the long series of 4—4—0s in Holland. They had Zara regulators and Knorr feed-water pumps and heaters.

174. 0—6—0 No. 3405 Class GO/2. Twenty of these engines were ordered from German builders for the Holland Railway Company, but by the time they were delivered in 1921 the Nederlandsche Spoorwegen was in being. Despite the similarity in appearance to the 4—4—0s of Class PO/2, boilers and other parts were not interchangeable. The Knorr feed-water pump and heater can be seen in this picture. ▼

▲175. British built W.D. Austerity 2—8—0 No. 4355 showing extension chimney. The N.S. had 237 of these engines and sold two to Sweden at the end of steam working in Holland.

▲176. Swedish-built three-cylinder 4—6—0 No. 4001. Like the 0—8—0 (above), these 15 engines were built by Nydquist & Holm to an existing design, in this case for the Bergslagernas Railway in 1930. Also like the 0—8—0s, they had bar frames and independent Walschaert valve gear for each valve, with roller bearings on all axles.

▲177. Swedish-built 3-cylinder 4—6—0 No.'4001. Fifteen engines were built by Nydquist & Holm for N.S. to the design of four Bergslagernas Railway (B.J.) Class Hz3 of 1927 which, however, had no smoke deflectors. The design included bar frames, individual Walschaerts gear for each valve and the N.S. engines had roller bearings for all axles.

178. 4—4—4T No. 5810, Class PTO/2 leaving Rotterdam with a train for Venlo. Twelve engines were built for the Holland Railway Company in 1914-15, being a larger version of preceding 4—4—2Ts. With many other tank engines, they survived until the last days of steam.

179. 4—6—4T No. 6019, Class PTO/3. These fine engines were introduced on the Netherlands State Railway in 1913 and 26 were built. During the Second War, several were sent to the S.N.C.F. and finished their lives in France. This post-war photograph shows No. 6019 at its last depot—Nijmegen.

180. Four-cylinder 4—6—4T No. 6108, Class PTO/4. Ten of these express tank engines were built in 1929, and were the tank engine version of the last five 4—6—0s of Class PO/3 (Plate 169). Boilers, cylinders, motion and many details were interchangeable.

181. 0—4—0T No. 8109, Class R/2—L/3. Introduced in 1901 on the Netherlands State Railway, these useful little engines were used both for shunting and for short hauls on branch lines—hence their double classification.

182. 0—6—0T No. 8513, Class RO/1. Nine of these engines were built without superheaters for the Netherlands State Railway in 1915 and a further six (of which No. 8513 is one) with superheaters, in 1920.

183. Four-cylinder 4—8—4T No. 6312, Class GTO/3. Twenty-two were built in 1930-31 for the South Limburg coal traffic and were the heaviest (126.4 *tonnes*) and most powerful European tank locomotives. With their tractive effort (70 per cent) of 32,340 lb, they were also the most powerful N.S. locomotives. They were the freight tank engine version of Class PO/4 (Plate 170) and one of them (number unknown) was the last locomotive in steam in Holland.

G

CORAS IOMPAIR EIREANN : C.I.E.

Gauge : 5ft 3in (1.60m)

The Great Southern Railway was formed in 1925 by an amalgamation of four large companies and several smaller ones, and it operated most of the broad gauge lines and some of the 3ft gauge lines in Eire. In 1945 nationalisation resulted in the G.S.R. and the Dublin United Transport Co. being taken over by the C.I.E.

The Great Northern Railway of Ireland remained independent until 1958, when its lines and property in Eire were absorbed into the C.I.E., and those in Northern Ireland by the Ulster Transport Authority (*q.v.*).

The first steam locomotives in Ireland ran on the Dublin and Kingstown Railway, opened in 1834 and which, until 1857, was 4ft 8½in gauge. It is probable that the first train was hauled by a 2—2—0 with two horizontal outside cylinders, named *Vauxhall* and built by Forrester of Liverpool in 1834. *Hibernia*, a 2—2—0 with two vertical cylinders built by Sharp Roberts, was also an early performer on the D.K.R.

Locomotive design in Ireland was always very similar to that in Great Britain, but full use was never made of the wide gauge to build locomotives of great power and four-coupled passenger and six-coupled freight engines were by far the most common. There was always great variety, new engines usually being built in small groups. In 1936, for example, eleven years after amalgamation, the G.S.R. owned 483 engines of 13 types and 75 classes. The largest group of locomotives were the 110 0—6—0s of Class J-15 built between 1866 and 1903 for the G.S. & W. In later years many were rebuilt and superheated, but engines of the original design were still at work during the last days of steam. The most powerful and most modern design in Ireland was that of the three three-cylinder 4—6—0s of Class B-1a built by the Great Southern at Inchicore in 1939–40.

The G.S. & W. Works at Inchicore have been the nursery of many famous locomotive engineers, notably Sir John Aspinall, H. A. Ivatt and R. E. L. Maunsell. After leaving the Southern Railway of England, O. V. S. Bulleid went to Inchicore and was able to continue his experiments with multi-cylinder locomotives and also to investigate the possibilities of peat as a locomotive fuel.

The most progressive and best administered of the Irish railways was the Great Northern, whose main line was the direct route between Belfast and Dublin. The G.N. engines were four-coupled for passenger and six-coupled for freight, but they were adequate for the jobs they had to do, and their performance was of a high order. In their blue livery the passenger locomotives made a handsome picture and the three-cylinder compound 4—4—0s and the later three-cylinder simples were among the finest looking of all European steam locomotives. There was a high degree of standardisation of boilers and parts on the G.N.R.(I)

In Eire, the present and future motive power is diesel, locomotives and multiple-unit railcars being used.

ULSTER TRANSPORT AUTHORITY : U.T.A.

The principal railways of Northern Ireland were the Northern Counties Committee (N.C.C.), Belfast & County Down (B.C.D.) and part of the Great Northern. The first two were nationalised in 1948 by the U.T.A., which, ten years later, absorbed the Great Northern lines in Northern Ireland. The major component of the U.T.A. was the N.C.C., which, as the Belfast & Northern Counties Railway (B.N.C.) had been bought by the Midland (of England) in 1903 and was then successively owned by the L.M.S. and the British Transport Commission, becoming then known as the Railway Executive (Northern Counties Committee). As well as its broad gauge lines, the N.C.C. operated 44 miles of 3ft gauge, which were closed to traffic soon after the Second War.

The locomotives taken over from the B.N.C. by the Midland were mostly two-cylinder compounds with inside cylinders. Some were later rebuilt as superheated simple engines, and the Midland built simple 4—4—0s for the express services and a few 0—6—0s for freight. Under L.M.S. ownership, the N.C.C. was modernised and standardised with some fine 2—6—0s and 2—6—4Ts, again with the stamp of Derby on their design. Two standard L.M.S. 0—6—0Ts for shunting were also sent over and altered to 5ft 3in gauge.

Engines of the Belfast & County Down were mainly 4—4—2T and 4—6—4T but all the locomotives of this railway were withdrawn by 1956 and most of the railway was closed to traffic. The G.N. engines in Northern Ireland were from the stock of that railway and U.T.A. ownership brought little alteration before scrapping.

The future motive power of the U.T.A. is diesel locomotives for freight and multiple-unit railcars for passenger duties.

184. Ex G.S. & W. 0—6—0s Nos. 166 and 109 Class J-15 on a train from Cork to Fermoy. No. 166 was rebuilt with a Z class superheater boiler but retained D slide valves. No. 109 was in her original form. The J-15s formed numerically the largest locomotive class in Ireland.

185. 4—4—0 No. 342 Class D-4 and 4—6—0 No. 409 Class B-2 on a Dublin to Cork express. No. 342 was one of five engines built at Inchicore in 1937, the design being similar to some earlier rebuilt engines. With tractive effort 18,000 lb, this was the most powerful 4—4—0 of the C.I.E. and bogie and tender axles had roller bearings.

186. 0—6—2T No. 673 Class I-3. Built at Inchicore in 1933-4 for the Dublin suburban services, there were five of these engines which had Class Z superheater boilers, the same as that used for the rebuilt J-15 (Plate 192).

187. Three-cylinder 4—6—0 Class B-1a No. 800 *Maeve*. Three engines were built 1939-40 and represented the furthest development of the steam locomotive in Ireland. In many characteristics, Class B-1a were similar to the Stanier rebuilt "Royal Scots" of the L.M.S., which they preceded. They set an entirely new pattern of motive power in Ireland, and their tractive effort of 33,000 lb was greatly in advance of that of any previous locomotive. The axle-load of 21 tons, however, limited their sphere of operation but they were built specifically to work the Dublin-Cork main line. They had double blast-pipes and chimneys and roller bearings to bogie and tender axles.

The first 4—6—0 in Ireland was built in 1916 at Inchicore, had four cylinders and was not superheated. Superheated versions were built later, and in 1932-36 all were reconstructed as two-cylinder simples and No. 409, the train engine shown in Plate 193, was one of these.

188. 2—6—0 No. 381, Class K-1, in its original form. The Maunsell Class N 2—6—0s went into service on the S.E. & C.R. in 1917. They were excellent modern engines with long-travel valves and coned Belpaire boilers. After the First War, to relieve both unemployment and the shortage of locomotives, Woolwich Arsenal built parts for the Class N which it was hoped main line companies would buy and erect in their own works. Apart from six bought by the Metropolitan Railway and built as 2—6—4Ts, the only English railway to buy parts was the S.E. & C. The M. & G.W. of Ireland bought parts for six engines in 1924, adapted them for 5ft 3in gauge and erected them at Broadstone Works. After 1925, the Great Southern bought a further 15 and in 1930 six more which were given 6ft 0in diameter wheels. (Class K-1a.) Until the advent of No. 800 (above) the Class K-1 were the most powerful locomotives in Ireland (T.E. 26,040 lb). They all received the wider standard G.S.R. chimneys and had extra snifting valves above the steam chests.

189. U.T.A. 4—4—0 No. 70, Class U-2 Nos. 70 and 71 were the first of the modern 4—4—0s, built by the Midland at Derby Works for the N.C.C. in 1914. They were Class U and had round-top superheated boilers. Two more were built in 1924 and there was an 0—6—0 goods engine version. Later that year came the U-2 Belpaire 4—4—0s and ultimately the original engines were all rebuilt to that class which, with 18 engines, was the most numerous on the N.C.C. All the U-2s had inside Walschaert gear.

190. U.T.A. 2—6—0 Class W No. 98 *King Edward VIII*. This was W. A. Stanier's 1933 design for the N.C.C., and four were built at Derby and eleven at Belfast during the following 10 years. They were derived from the Fowler 2—6—4Ts of the L.M.S. but had 6ft driving wheels and wider fireboxes.

191. U.T.A. 2—6—4T No. 4, Class WT. Ten were built at Derby in 1946-7. They were the tank engine version of the 2—6—0s (above).

192. G.N.R. 4—4—2T No. 187, Class T-1. Introduced in 1913 for the Belfast and Dublin suburban services, five were built without superheaters. A further 20 were built 1921-29 and these were Class T-2. They had superheaters and slightly larger tanks; all the 4—4—2Ts had bogie brakes and the T-1s were later superheated. They were excellent and economical engines and a tender engine version (Class U) was introduced in 1915.

193. G.N.R. 0—6—4T No. 22, Class RT. Four of these engines were built, two each in 1908 and 1911 for interchange traffic from Belfast docks. They were not superheated.

194. G.N.R. 0—6—0 No. 80, Class UG. Introduced in 1937, these were the most modern freight engines on the Great Northern. They were used extensively also as mixed-traffic engines and with a 15¾-ton axle-load they had a high route availability. The boiler, cylinders and motion were interchangeable with those of the 4—4—2Ts and the 4—4—0s of Class U (Plate 191).

195. G.N.R. three-cylinder 4—4—0 Class VS No. 208 *Lagan*. In 1932 five three-cylinder Smith compound 4—4—0s went into service on the Belfast-Dublin express services. The compound system was that of the Midland in England but the B.P. was originally 250 lb/sq in. In 1948 the five three-cylinder simple 4—4—0s of Class VS were built and the boilers were interchangeable with those of the compounds. The pressure was 220 lb/sq in and the engines had three sets of Walschaerts gear. They were imposing and beautiful machines and the most powerful G.N. express engines.

196. G.N.R. 4—4—0 Class U No. 204 *Antrim*. Another modern and beautiful design was this lightweight 4—4—0 of Class U, five of which went into service in 1948. They were a modernised and slightly heavier version of an earlier (1915) design (also Class U) and were the passenger counterparts of Class UG (Plate 189) with a similar axle loading. The tenders ran on roller bearings.

ITALIAN STATE RAILWAYS
Ferrovie dello Stato: F.S.
Gauge : 4ft 8½ in (1.435m)
3ft 1⅜in (0.95m)

Three large private companies were amalgamated and taken over by the State in 1905 to form the Italian State Railways. The first steam locomotive was an inside-cylinder 2—2—2 named *Bayard*, built by Longridge & Co., Newcastle, being their No. 120 of 1839. It was similar to their No. 119 built for Holland (page 87) but the Italian engine ran on the standard gauge. *Bayard* pulled the first train from Naples to Portici on 3rd October, 1839.

Italy was one of the earliest European countries to adopt electric traction, as she has ample water power for generating stations in the North and is within easy reach of oil fuel in the South. She has always been very short of coal, and until the enforcing of sanctions against her in 1936, relied largely on supplies from Britain.

Locomotive design often reflected the need for coal economy, and compound locomotives of several types were built, but were finally rejected or converted to simples. Several examples of the Plancher four-cylinder compound 0—10—0s, however, remained in service until the last days of steam (Plate 204). Introduced in 1907 for mountain freight duties and for banking, these engines originally had a separate tender but coal was carried in a side bunker. In the Plancher system the two H.P. cylinders (one inside and one outside the frames) with their common piston valve were on the R.H. side and the two similarly disposed L.P. cylinders were on the L.H. side of the engines. The cut-off could be made combined or independent by the engagement or disengagement of two toothed wheels on the reverser in the cab.

No steam locomotive development occurred in Italy after 1930 but some outstanding modifications were made to existing types, and were adopted in the designs of many locomotives all over the world.

Poppet valves of the Caprotti type, which were first applied to an F.S. locomotive in 1921, were the idea of an Italian motor engineer and were successful, particularly in modified form, greatly improving the steam distribution and therefore the economy of F.S. locomotives.

Undoubtedly the most controversial of all fuel economy measures, adopted in 1937 by the Italian Railways, was the Franco-Crosti boiler, in which the flue gases and exhaust steam are led back from the smokebox through two economisers, to exhaust from two laterally placed chimneys in front of the cab (Plates 202 and 203). A modified form with a single economiser (the Crosti boiler) has been used for the F.S. 2—8—0s of Group 741 (Plate 207) and in some other countries, notably Britain, Germany and Spain (*q.v.*). The final low temperature and lowered velocity of the smokebox gases at exhaust allowed the formation of sulphuric acid which caused severe corrosion of economiser tubes and other parts of the system. The Italians always claimed that they suffered only slightly from this trouble and that it occurred mostly at the chimney top, a claim which was, in turn, doubted and explained by the use on the F.S. of British coal with a very low sulphur content. Chrome steel was, however, used for the chimneys of some Crosti engines.

Many Italian locomotive designs included the Zara, or "Italian truck" in which the leading radial wheels and the leading coupled wheels form a bogie and are mounted in a separate frame which is pivoted in such a manner as to allow most side-play in the radial wheels and less in the leading coupled wheels. Engines to which this truck was fitted included all 2—6—0, 2—6—2, 2—8—0 and 2—10—0 types and their tank engine equivalents except those of foreign origin.

Apart from some main lines all the routes of the F.S. are laid with comparatively light rail and 16½ *tonnes* was the maximum axle load for general purpose steam locomotives. Only on a small number of main line locomotives was this limit exceeded. In order to get maximum power for minimum axle loading, a number of locomotives were built with the lightest possible plate frames and with inside cylinders having piston valves outside the frames. There were 2—6—0s and 2—8—0 mixed traffic engines with this arrangement. The largest Italian passenger locomotives were the four-cylinder Pacifics of Group 691 (Plate 197) and the largest freight engines were eighteen two-cylinder simple 2—10—0s of Group 480 designed for the Brenner line but which spent most of their lives in Sicily (Plate 205). Neither was outstanding by modern standards. Although the first European 4—8—0 appeared in Italy in 1902, no engines of this wheel arrangement remained in the last days of steam.

As a result of the Wars the F.S. absorbed into its stock a large number of foreign engines, the most prolific being various Austrian types, notably Südbahn 2—10—0s and Göldsdorf 0—10—0 two-cylinder compounds. The several German types included many of the ubiquitous Prussian 0—8—0s of Types G-8 and G-8/1. After the Second War, 243 U.S. Army 2—8—0s (Plate 160) were taken over by the F.S. and equipped for burning oil fuel.

The present and future motive power in Italy is electric using 3,000 volts D.C., overhead conduction. This has now almost entirely replaced earlier three-phase A.C. electrification. Diesel-hydraulic and diesel-electric locomotives and diesel-hydraulic and diesel-mechanical railcars and train sets are used on non-electrified lines.

197. Four-cylinder 4—6—2 No. 691.031. These 33 engines were 1928-33 rebuilds of 1911 Pacifics of Group 690; as rebuilt, the boilers were interchangeable with those of Group 746 (below). The four cylinders had common piston valves for each pair and all drove the middle coupled axle. The sandbox was located around the steam dome a usual feature of Italian locomotives. A 19-*tonne* axle-load limited their duties to a few main lines, e.g., Venice—Rome and Venice—Udine. They were sluggish, though powerful machines with short-travel valves.

198. Four-cylinder compound 2—8—2 No. 746.015. Fifty were built in 1922. The H.P. cylinders were inside and the L.P. outside; all drove the third coupled axle. Each set of Walschaert gear drove one H.P. and one L.P. valve, the drive for the former being taken off the combination lever; the L.P. cut-off was always 12-15 per cent greater than the H.P. In 1926 ten were built with Caprotti valves. An axle loading of only 16½ *tonnes* gave Group 746 a wide range of usefulness, but they were indifferent performers.

199. 2—6—0s Nos. 640.018 and 640.094. Light passenger engines with outside piston valves and a leading Italian truck, introduced in 1907. They had a separate sandbox on the boiler and Coale safety valves immediately behind the dome. They were quiet-running and economical engines. In 1927-32, 16 earlier but similar two-cylinder compounds were rebuilt as two-cylinder simples with Caprotti valves and included in Group 640, 3XX.

200. 2—8—0 No. 745.049 leaving Padova with a train for Calalzo. Light mixed-traffic engines introduced in 1914 for heavily graded lines laid with light track. They suffered from having too small big-end bearings; later but similar engines (Group 744) built in 1927 had outside cylinders and valves.

201 and 202. The four-cylinder 2—6—2s of Group 685 were the F.S. standard express locomotives built between 1912 and 1927. They had Italian trucks and a 15-*tonne* axle-load and the earlier engines had Walschaert gear driving two piston valves for the four cylinders. **Plate 201** (upper) shows No. 685.103. Many of these engines were later rebuilt with Caprotti valves. Some earlier four-cylinder Plancher compound 2—6—2s of Groups 680 (saturated) and 681 (superheated) were rebuilt as simples of Group 685, some with piston valves and others with Caprotti valves. Some of the Caprotti rebuilds had feed-water pumps and heaters, trefoil blast-pipes and a higher working pressure and these were Group S685. In 1927 the last of the Group 685 were built—30 engines, all with Caprotti valves, and in 1940 five of these were rebuilt with Franco-Crosti boilers, water treatment plant and streamlining, to become Group 683. **Plate 202** (lower) shows No. 683.981 leaving Mestre with the Simplon-Orient Express.

203. 2—6—0 No. 623.446 with a van train near Venice. This was one of 35 given Franco-Crosti boilers in 1952-3. It was originally a two-cylinder compound of Group 600 but was one of 156 rebuilt as a simple with Caprotti valves in the mid-nineteen-twenties. These rebuilds became part of Group 625, which until then consisted only of two-cylinder simple 2—6—0s with outside piston valves built 1910-23, some of which were among the 35 which received Franco-Crosti boilers (Group 623).

204. Four-cylinder Plancher compound 0—10—0 No. 471.019. Being balanced compounds with cranks at 180° the exhaust was only two beats for each revolution of the wheels. They were built without superheaters as Group 470.

205. 2—10—0 No. 480.005. With a tractive effort of 40,486 lb, these were the most powerful locomotives in Italy.

206. 2—8—0 No. 740.261. Standard F.S. freight engine, of which 470 were built between 1911 and 1923. A few had Caprotti valves. There were three different types of blast-pipes and chimneys, the engine illustrated having a wide chimney, a "razor" in the blast-pipe and a steel firebox.

207. 2—8—0 No. 741.110. This was one of 81 engines of Group 740 rebuilt with Crosti boilers in the mid-nineteen-fifties. Note the Davies & Metcalfe exhaust steam injector. Earlier (1942-53) 94 of Group 740 were rebuilt with Franco-Crosti boilers with two economisers.

208. 2—8—0 No. 735.333. During the First War, 400 were built in America with the same dimensions as Group 740. They had bar frames and most of the typical Italian features were missing. During the last days of steam in Italy, 40 were sold to Greece.

209. 2—6—0T No. 875.039. The F.S. had 117 of these little branch-line engines built 1912-1916. Later engines were built with superheater and piston valves and some of Group 875 were rebuilt to this Group 880.

210. 0—6—0T No. 835.052. There were 370 of these standard shunting tanks built from 1906 to 1922 The frames and wheels from some of them were used in the construction of electric shunting engines of the same wheel arrangement.

211. 0—8—0WT No. 896.015. Standard super-heater heavy shunting engine introduced in 1921. Similar saturated engines with slide valves (Group 895) were built first in 1909.

212. No. 200.04, one of four 0—4—0T built in 1883 by Marcinelle et Couillet and used for shunting at the Milan terminus of the railway.

Ferrovie Nord Milano

Gauge : 4ft 8½in (1.435m)

This is the largest and most important standard gauge private railway in Europe. It was projected by a Belgian engineer and the first section from Milan to Saronno was opened in 1879. It connects Milan with the principal Italian lakes but also runs to Novara. It is now completely electrified using 3,000 volts D.C., overhead conduction. Before electrification it was operated entirely by tank engines, using 0—4—0T, 0—6—0T, 0—8—0T, 4—6—0T, 2—8—0T and three-cylinder 2—6—4T. The last two types were very large and imposing machines, but the last survivors of steam on the Nord Milan were 0—8—0T, 0—4—0T and 4—6—0T.

213. No. 280.17, one of eighteen passenger 4—6—0 well-tank engines built by German and Italian builders between 1909 and 1927.

LUXEMBOURG NATIONAL RAILWAYS COMPANY
Société Nationale des Chemins de Fer Luxembourgeois: C.F.L.

Gauge : 4ft 8½in (1.435m)

The first railway in the Grand Duchy of Luxembourg was opened on 4th October, 1859, and connected Arlon (in Belgium) via Luxembourg City with Thionville in France. It was called the Société Royale Grand Ducale des Chemins de Fer Guillaume—Luxembourg (G–L) and was operated by the French Chemins de Fer de l'Est, who ran the first trains. Particulars of the first locomotives to run in Luxembourg have not been recorded.

After the defeat of France by Germany in 1870 other lines of the G–L were completed and were operated by the Sarrebrück Division of the Prussian State Railway, and in 1873 another railway, the Société Prince-Henri (P–H) opened lines which crossed the country East to West via Ettelbruck and connected Germany with Belgium and North East France. After various changes of ownership by France, Belgium, Alsace-Lorraine and Germany the two Companies were amalgamated in 1946 to form the C.F.L., 51 per cent of which is vested in Luxembourg and 24½ per cent each in Belgium and France.

The city of Luxembourg forms a hub for five main lines which radiate East to Treves and Germany, South East to Thionville and Metz, South West to Longwy and Paris, West to Arlon and Brussels, and North to Liège. The Grand Duchy itself forms an integral and important part of one of the world's richest iron-ore areas and with the adjacent lands of the Saar, Eastern France and the South of Belgium forms the greatest steel producing area of Europe. The C.F.L. is therefore mainly concerned with the transport of iron-ore, coal, and their resulting products. The steam locomotives have always been mostly heavy freight types and their pattern mostly German. Only the Prince Henri Railway developed some original designs, though it made distinctive modifications to the German types which it ordered.

After both Wars the railways of Luxembourg received their quota of Prussian and Reichsbahn types, and alone of the countries of Western Europe purchased ten of the "Liberation" type locomotives built in England.

The main lines of the C.F.L. will, in future, be electrified using 25 kV monophase 50-cycle A.C., except for the Luxembourg-Arlon line which uses 3,000 volts D.C. Diesel-electric locomotives and diesel-mechanical railcars deal with traffic on other non-electric lines.

214. Cab side of No. 5513 (German Type 42) gives the following information:

(i) the engine belongs to Bettembourg shed.

(ii) R below the number means *rechauffé*—fitted with feed-water heater.

(iii) the three coloured discs below the number show:
   (a) T.I.A. (water treatment),
   (b) the percentage tin in the white metal of bearings,
   (c) steel firebox.

(iv) information showing weights empty and in working order, brake-weights and date of last overhaul. Information is given about the tender weights and capacity on the tank side (bottom left).

215. 0—10—0 No. 5222, ex-Prussian State Class G-10, introduced 1910. Four went to the G-L after the First War. Although not so common as the Prussian G-8 0—8—0s, more than 2,500 of the Class G-10 were built and as a result of the two wars were to be found in Austria, France, Italy, Holland, Norway and other countries. On the G-L they were given modified cabs and A.C.F.I. feed pumps and heaters with a top-feed dome. Two square sand-boxes were mounted on the boiler. The P-H purchased eleven similar engines new from German builders in 1913-21, P-H Class K, which had bell-mouthed chimneys and only one sand-box. They were 8 *tonnes* heavier than the Prussian engines. All the 0—10—0s had side-play in the first and fifth axles.

216. Three-cylinder 2—10—0 No. 5301. This was a development of the Prussian G-12 (Plate 93) but with smaller driving wheels and cylinders, bar frames and wide fireboxes with hollow stays. All three cylinders drove the third coupled axle. Fifteen were built by Henschel in 1916-17, ten for Turkey and five for the Prussian State Railways. After the First War, three of the latter went to Belgium and then to the P-H to become their Class O-1. They acquired bell-mouthed chimneys and A.C.F.I. pumps and heaters. Both the G-L and the P-H had some of the later bar-framed G-12s (18 each) after the First War and four were built new by Borsig in 1918 for the P-H and were their Class O. ▼

▲217. 2—8—0 No. 4710 on a Luxembourg—Rodange train leaving Bettembourg. After the Second War in 1946, the C.F.L. purchased 10 "Liberation" class locomotives from the Vulcan Foundry. These engines were additional to the 110 built by Vulcan for U.N.R.R.A. for service in the Soviet European Colonies. They were powerful machines with a maximum axle-load of 18.5 tons. The firebox was of copper and had three arch tubes.

218. 2—10—0 No. 5605 with an express from Liege near Luxembourg. The C.F.L. obtained two series of German 2—10—0s after the Second War. Type 52 became C.F.L. Series 56. Ten of these were part of a batch of 100 built in Belgium immediately after the War, the other 90 becoming S.N.C.B. Type 26 (Page 16). The remaining ten C.F.L. engines were built by Grafenstaden in 1947. The second series of post war 2—10—0s were German Type 42 (Plate 9), twenty of which came to the C.F.L. as their Series 55 from Austrian builders (Florisdorf 1944-48). ▼

219. 2—6—2T No. 3410, P-H Class H-1, and 2—6—0T No. 3023, ex-Prussian Class T-9. Three series of very characteristic 2—6—2 passenger tanks were built for the P-H, and after the formation of the C.F.L. they dealt with most of the local passenger services as well as the lighter main-line expresses. No. 3410 was one of ten very pretty little engines which came from La Meuse in 1913.

220. 2—6—2T No. 3512, P-H Class L. This was a later, heavier and more powerful type than Class H-1, and thirteen were built by Jung during the First War. This example carried A.C.F.I. feed pump and heater, a turbo-generator for electric lighting and a "cistern" on top of the boiler for feed water treatment—altogether something of a "plumber's nightmare" which did nothing to improve the appearance of an otherwise smart-looking engine.

221. 2—4—2T No. 2002 P-H Class E was built for local passenger services in 1900 and ended its days as shed pilot at Luxembourg.

222. 0—8—0T No. 4201, P-H Class G-1, was one of three superheated shunting engines built by Borsig in 1906.

223. 0—8—0T No. 4001, P-H Class G, shunting at Rodange with a typical background of blast furnaces. Class G consisted of three non-superheated engines with slide valves and smaller cylinders than those of the G-1.

NORWEGIAN STATE RAILWAYS
Norges Statsbaner: N.S.B.

Gauge : 4ft 8½in (1.435m)

The Norwegian Railways were financed and owned by the State from very early in their history, although the first railway in Norway, completed in 1854 between Christiania (Oslo) and Eidsvoll was privately financed by a British firm with Robert Stephenson as the engineer. This railway, the Norske Hoved Jernbane (Norwegian Trunk Line) was independent until 1926, when it was taken over by the N.S.B. Several classes of its locomotives remained until the last days of steam. They were of different design from those of the N.S.B., many having been built by Baldwin; they could often be identified by their oval number-plates.

The first steam locomotive to run in Norway was an outside cylinder 2—4—0 built by Robert Stephenson in 1851. It hauled the first train between Christiania and Eidsvoll on 1st September, 1854.

The steam locomotive in Norway did its difficult job well, often under extreme climatic conditions and with a number of severe limitations on its design. The requirements for Norwegian steam locomotives may be summarised as follows:

1. The engines had to be capable of climbing long gradients (the ruling gradient is 1 in 46) and of negotiating sharp curves. Many Norwegian lines were laid to metre gauge and were converted to standard gauge later. Hence the inheritance of many difficult and tortuous routes.

2. They had to be reliable and above all, economical in service. No coal is mined in Norway and imported Polish, German or Silesian soft coal was always very expensive.

3. A maximum axle-load of only 16 tons was allowed and on many lines it was even less than this. On the other hand, the loading gauge allowed a height of 13ft 9½in and a width overall of 11ft 2in.

4. High speeds were not possible anywhere in Norway, and the maximum of 100 Km/hr (62 m.p.h.) was permitted only on comparatively few lines. Fortunately train loads never exceeded 375 *tonnes* for a single engine —heavier loads being double-headed.

Surprisingly, articulated engines were never used on the Norwegian Railways and during the last days of steam the types on the main lines were 2—8—0, 4—8—0, 2—8—4 and 2—10—0 while 2—6—0, 4—6—0 and 2—6—2T were the common branch-line engines. It was usual for there to be a light and a heavy version of each type, the former being similar in appearance, but smaller than the latter. In many types there were compound and simple versions, *e.g.*, there were two-cylinder compound 2—6—0s and 2—6—2Ts working alongside similar engines with two simple cylinders. Among the 4—6—0s and the 4—8—0s were many four-cylinder simples but the preference was generally for the later four-cylinder compound versions of these engines. In all four-cylinder engines, with the exception of the 2—8—4s, a common piston valve was used for each pair of cylinders; in the compounds there was one valve for the inside H.P. and outside L.P. cylinder of each side. In the simples, a common piston valve involved the use of crossed ports.

The majority of Norwegian locomotives were built in Oslo by Thunes Mekaniske Vaerksted, other engines being built mainly by Nydquist & Holm and by German and Swiss builders. As a result of German occupation during the Second War, the N.S.B. had 69 2—10—0s of the German Type 52 (Plate 312) built between 1942 and 1944 in Germany, and six 0—10—0s of Prussian Class G-10 (Plate 215). The Germans also put into service four further four-cylinder compound 2—8—4s. The design was modified from that of the first three engines, and two were built by Thunes and two by Krupp.

The numerical classification was followed for Norwegian steam locomotives, classes up to 49 being N.S.B. engines and classes 50 to 63 applying to engines absorbed from private lines (excluding the Hoved Jernbane) and to the German engines; the G-10s became Class 61a and the 52s Class 63a. Most N.S.B. engines were ordered in twos and threes and they were numbered accordingly. There were few long runs of numbers in a class.

The main lines of the N.S.B. will, in future, be electrified using single phase A.C., 15 kV 16⅔ cycles. On non-electrified lines, diesel-electric locomotives are used and diesel railcars and train sets satisfactorily deal with many of the passenger services.

224. Four-cylinder compound 2—8—4 No. 472 Class 49c. The three original 2—8—4s (Nos. 463/4/5) were built by Thunes in 1935-6, the first being named *Dovregubben* (Dovre Giant), the engines all being built for the Dovre line between Trondheim and Dombås. The first two engines were Class 49a and the third was 49b and was fitted with a booster on the trailing four-wheeled truck. This was later removed. The leading radial wheel and the leading coupled wheel were in a separate frame forming a Zara or Italian truck (Page 100). These three engines had double blast-pipes and chimneys. In 1940, during the German occupation, two engines were delivered by Krupp (Nos. 470/1) and a further two from Thunes (Nos. 472/3). These later engines were Class 49c and they had single blast-pipes, smaller H.P. cylinders and other minor differences from the earlier engines. The maximum axle-load was 15.6 *tonnes*, a remarkable figure for an engine capable of developing 2,600 H.P. With this low adhesive weight, careful driving was necessary to prevent slipping, and two large sand-boxes can be seen on top of the boiler. The L.P. cylinders were outside and the valves were driven by Heusinger gear, the inside H.P. valves being driven through rocking shafts. The engines were hand-fired and the frameless Vanderbilt tenders had retractable wooden covers over the bunker to prevent the coal freezing.

225. View from the footplate of 2—8—4 No. 473 at the summit of the line over the Dovre Mountain. The barren windswept tundra is cold and desolate even in the summer.

226. 4—6—0 No. 304 Class 27. Seventeen of these two-cylinder simple engines were built between 1910 and 1921. Individual engines varied in detail. The dome, with safety valves on top, was in the same cover as the sand-box—a common Scandinavian practice. The extraordinary smoke deflectors were devised at Hamar, most Norwegian motive power districts having their own ideas on this subject. It was commonly stated that engines without any such deflectors had least trouble from steam drifting down! The white line on the deflectors shows the centre line of the chimney.

227. Four-cylinder 4—6—0 No. 279, Class 30a, with a Trondheim—Oslo Express leaving Otta. Engines of this type with the four-cylinder compound variants of Class 30b were built between 1914 and 1939. All had two piston valves for the four cylinders.

228. Four-cylinder compound 4—8—0 No. 437, Class 26c, on a south-bound freight at Otta. The first 4—8—0s in Norway were four-cylinder simples of Class 26a built in Switzerland in 1910. Class 26c were compounds, seventeen being built between 1919 and 1924. These classes were light 4—8—0s having a maximum axle-load of only 11.6 *tonnes*.

229. Four-cylinder compound 4—8—0 No. 419, Class 31b, with a Bergen—Oslo express at Voss. Twenty-two of these heavy 4—8—0s (axle-load 14 *tonnes*) were built for the Bergen line in 1921-6 and they succeeded five similar simples built in 1915 (Class 31a). The bars in front of the spectacles protected the glass from frozen snow.

230. 2—10—0 No. 308 working a freight train on the Bergen—Oslo line. The line which carries the heaviest traffic in Scandinavia is the iron-ore line which runs between Kiruna in Sweden and Narvik on the coast of Norway. It was electrified in 1923. For working the heavy ore-trains, seven 0—10—0s were built from 1913-1920 and after electrification these engines came south. Their axle-load was, however, 16.2 *tonnes* and so they were rebuilt as 2—10—0s, the frames being lengthened and the boiler moved forward. As a result the axle loading was reduced to 15 *tonnes* and the engines all worked freight on the Bergen line. They were all fitted with counter-pressure braking, the silencers for which were located around the chimney and resulted in what was, externally, the widest locomotive chimney in Europe.

231. 2—8—0 No. 301, Class 33a, on a freight train for Bergen passing Nesttun. Built between 1919 and 1921 these were the most modern of several classes of 2—8—0. They were straight-forward two-cylinder engines of which 14 were built and worked on the Kiruna—Narvik line before electrification.

▲ **232.** Two-cylinder compound 2—6—0 No. 183, Class 21a, with a Bergen suburban train at Nesttun. An early 2—6—0 introduced in 1905. As with all the compounds, a change valve allowed live steam at reduced pressure into the L.P. cylinder for starting.

233. Two-cylinder simple 2—6—0 No. 224, Class 21b. This was one of the largest group of tender engines on the N.S.B., 33 being built from 1919. They had a 10-*tonne* axle-load and were ideal engines for lightly-laid branch lines.
▼

234. Superheated 0—6—0 well and side tank No. 424, Class 25d. Thirty-five 0—6—0 tanks were the standard shunting engines, the first being built in Switzerland, which accounts for their close resemblance to similar engines on the S.B.B. (Plate 300).

235. Baldwin 2—3—2T No. 328, Class 34a, was one of three built in 1918 for the Hoved Jernbane.

236. 2—6—2T No. 331, Class 32c, with a suburban train at Bergen. There were 24 of these engines built between 1915 and 1921, some for the Hoved Jernbane. They varied in detail.

PORTUGUESE RAILWAY COMPANY
Companhia do Caminhos de Ferro Portugueses: C.P.

Gauges : 5ft 5 $\frac{9}{16}$ in (1.665m)

3ft 3 $\frac{3}{8}$ in (1.0m)

Until 1927 about half of the broad-gauge lines in Portugal were owned and operated by the Companhia do Caminhos de Ferro Portugueses (C.P.), a company largely financed in France, which had been formed in 1860 and had built the main Lisbon–Oporto line. Most of the other lines were state-owned, the most important being the Sul e Sueste (S.S.) south of the Tagus, and the Minho e Douro (M.D.) to the north and east of Oporto. This latter railway had also a considerable mileage of metre gauge feeder lines running down the valleys to the Douro line. There were several other independent metre-gauge lines, as well as the important broad gauge Beira Alta.

On 11th May, 1927, the C.P. obtained a lease to operate all the State-owned railways, both broad and metre gauge, but a year later the C.P. leased its metre gauge lines to two independent railways, the Northern of Portugal and the National Railways Company. In 1948, however, the C.P. obtained a concession to lease all the broad and metre gauge lines, including the Beira Alta and the metre gauge Vale do Vouga, and now it operates all the Portuguese railways with the single exception of the short electrified Estoril Railway, which still retains its independence.

The first railway in Portugal was built with British capital by the Companhia Penninsular dos Caminhos de Ferro de Portugal. The gauge was 1.435m (4ft 8½in), and the line was opened between Lisbon and Carregado on 28th October, 1856. A 2—2—2 locomotive with outside cylinders hauled the first train but no particulars of this locomotive are available. In 1859 the broad gauge of 1.665m was adopted, this being ⅜in narrower than that of the Spanish railways. Through working between the two systems is, however, possible.

Even during the last days of steam in Portugal there were many different types and classes of locomotives at work, some of them very old and many dating from the earlier years of the present century. Most of the more recent types were of German construction. It was quite usual to see modern diesel-electrics side-by-side with 70-year-old steam locomotives.

In the early nineteen-sixties, trains on the main line between Lisbon and Oporto used three forms of motive power: from Lisbon to Entroncamento monophase, 50-cycle A.C. electric; from Entroncamento to Villa Nova de Gaia diesel-electric; and from Villa Nova de Gaia to Oporto steam locomotives (often very ancient) took the trains across the high Eiffel bridge over the Douro, which for years was not strong enough to carry the heavy diesel-electrics.

In a country short of coal it is not surprising that many locomotives were compounds, and that after the Second War, many engines were oil-fired. The largest numerical group of engines were four-cylinder compound 4—6—0s of three classes (page 121). All were de Glehn-du Bousquet compounds with outside H.P. cylinders and independent cut-off for H.P. and L.P. cylinders. They had change valves to admit live steam at reduced pressure to the L.P. cylinders for starting. There were also two classes of two-cylinder simple 4—6—0s, one with inside and the other with outside cylinders and both originating on the Sul e Sueste (Southern & South Eastern) Division of the State Railways. The 4—6—0s did most of the work on semi-fast and local passenger trains, while two series of four-cylinder compound Pacifics were on express duties south of the Tagus.

Freight duties were mostly carried out by 2—8—0s and American-built 2—8—2s, even over the electrified lines, though 4—6—0s and 4—8—0s often took their turn as passenger trains were increasingly diesel-hauled.

Old six-coupled tender and tank engines were at work on local freight and shunting duties at a late date, and plenty of work was found for the more modern 2—6—4, 2—8—2 and 2—8—4 tank engines.

On the metre-gauge lines, the standardisation of motive power was much further advanced than on the broad gauge, though the locomotives were generally of much greater interest. The outstanding designs were undoubtedly the compound Mallet tank engines and the fine 2—8—2T, which came from the Northern of Portugal. All the metre-gauge locomotives were side tanks, and all had outside cylinders.

On the broad gauge lines, the future motive power is electric, working on the monophase, 50-cycle, 25kV, A.C., system. The Lisbon–Oporto main line is so far scheduled for electrification. Elsewhere diesel-electric locomotives, diesel railcars and some high speed Fiat diesel mechanical train sets will deal with the traffic. On the metre gauge lines the future is in diesel traction.

237. Four-cylinder compound 4—6—0 No. 270 with a local train from Oporto at Coimbra-B. These engines were built for the C.P. between 1899 and 1904 by the Cie. Fives—Lille and their similarity to contemporary engines on the C. de F. du Nord is obvious. They had slide valves to all cylinders.

238. Four-cylinder compound 4—6—0 No. 355 on a train from Coimbra to Oporto. Twenty were built for the C.P. between 1906 and 1913 by Henschel and the Société Alsacienne. They had piston valves for the H.P. cylinders.

239. Four-cylinder compound 4—6—0 No. 235 on a Douro line train from Oporto at Livraçao. Engines of this design formed the largest group of 4—6—0s in Portugal. They were built from 1903 to 1926 for both the Sul e Sueste (S.S.) and the Minho e Douro (M.D.) Divisions of the State Railways. They had Walschaert gear for the piston valves of the outside H.P. cylinders and Joy gear for the slide valves of the L.P. cylinders. When built they had copper-topped chimneys.

240. Oil-burning four-cylinder compound 4—6—2 No. 553. Ten were built by Henschel in 1924 for the S.S. Division of the State Railways. For many years these were the principal express locomotives south of the Tagus and were easily recognised by their four domes, the first and third being sand-boxes, the second a top-feed dome and the fourth containing the regulator. The H.P. cylinders were outside and the cut-off to H.P. and L.P. was independent.

241. Oil-burning four-cylinder compound 4—6—2 No. 502. Eight engines were built by Henschel in 1925 for the C.P. lines between Lisbon and Oporto. They were very similar to the S.S. engines (above), having the same cylinder and driving-wheel dimensions, but the boilers were different and were also higher pitched in the C.P. engines. With the same pressure, however, the tractive effort was the same for both classes. The C.P. engines could be recognised by having only one sand-box, and the drive being from the left-hand side. In both classes slide valves were used for the L.P. cylinders and piston valves for the H.P.

242. Four-cylinder compound 2—8—0 No. 763 with a west-bound freight train at Regua on the Douro line. These American-looking machines were introduced by the M.D. in 1912, the first four being built by the North British Locomotive Company and a further twelve by German builders, the last in 1926. They had bar frames and coned boilers and some had diamond-framed tender bogies. Walschaert gear drove two common piston valves, the L.P. cylinders being outside. They were not superheated.

243. Oil-burning two-cylinder simple 2—8—0 No. 707 at Regua, with a metre-gauge 2—4—6—0T on the left. Nineteen of these 2—8—0s were built for the Sul e Sueste Division of the State Railways between 1912 and 1921. They were superheated, had plate frames and originally had copper-topped chimneys.

244. Four-cylinder compound 4—8—0 No. 803. The most remarkable locomotives in Portugal were undoubtedly these big compounds, of which three were built by Henschel in 1931 for the heavily graded main line of the Beira Alta Railway. This line ran between the Spanish frontier at Vilar Formoso and the C.P. main line at Pampilhosa. They had bar frames and the boiler was pitched high to enable the grate to clear the two rear coupled axles. An A.C.F.I. feed pump and heater was fitted, and the safety valves were of the Coale type. The H.P. cylinders were outside and drove the second coupled axle while the inside, and steeply inclined, L.P. cylinders drove the leading axle. Compounding was on the de Glehn system with independent cut-off and four sets of Walschaert gear. The Kylchap double blast-pipes and chimneys were fitted later, the engines being built with single blast pipes. Despite their great size, the maximum axle-load was only 14.5 *tonnes* and the tractive effort at 50 per cent boiler pressure was 13,100 Kg. (28,880 lb).

245. Oil-burning 2—8—2 No. 872. Twenty engines were built by Alco 1944-5 and went to work on the main lines of the C.P. They were typical bar-framed American products and similar engines were supplied to several other countries. The maximum axle-load was 16.95 *tonnes*.

246. 0—6—0 No. 23. One of the oldest engines at work in Portugal in the last days of steam was this 0—6—0, which was built by Beyer Peacock in 1875 for the State-owned Minho & Douro Railway. It retained most of its original characteristics.

247. 4—8—0 No. 834. Six engines were built in Spain for the Sul e Sueste Division of the C.P. in 1947 and were the last steam locomotives built for Portugal. They were identical with the M.Z.A. 1400 Class introduced in 1918 and R.E.N.F.E. Nos. 240.2241—2425. Worthington feed pump and heaters were fitted to the Portuguese engines and they had left-hand drive.▼

248. 2—6—2T No. 039 with a local train at Coimbra-B. These nine little engines were built by Beyer Peacock in 1891 as 0—6—2T and were rebuilt for the C.P. in the form shown, in Lisbon between 1923 and 1930. New and bigger Belpaire boilers were fitted but the cylinders and motion remained untouched. The extra water tank in front and at the sides of the smoke-box provided weight for the leading radial wheel.

249. 2—6—2T No. 041. Two were built by Cockerill in 1908 for the Oporto suburban services of the Minho & Douro lines. They had slide valves and were not superheated.

250. 0—6—2T No. 011. This class was introduced on the State-owned Minho & Douro Railway in 1889 and four were built. They were freight tank engines used for shunting in the Oporto area.

251. Oil-burning 2–8–4T No. 0224 leaving the yards at Entroncamento with a freight train for Oporto. The C.P. owned 24 of these big tanks, which came from Henschel in 1924. Another ten engines of the same type but considerably smaller and less powerful were built during the same year, also by Henschel, for the S.S. Division of the State Railways.

252. Oil-burning 2—6—4T No. 071. Twenty-eight of these smart tank engines were built for the C.P., the first by Winterthur in 1916 and the last by Gerais of Lisbon in 1944. They worked the Lisbon and Oporto suburban services and semi-fast trains on the main line between these cities. A well tank was fitted between the frames in addition to the side tanks, and the water capacity was 2,198 gallons.

253. 2—6—0T No. E84. There were 22 2—6—0T on the metre-gauge, these being the most numerous type of locomotive. There were four classes, built between 1884 and 1910. No. E84 was built for the Minho & Douro Division of the State Railway by Kessler in 1886, and had Allen link motion. When the C.P. took over, all metre-gauge engines had the letter E before the number, ESTREITA, meaning *narrow*.

254. 2—8—2T No. E141. This was one of four engines built by Henschel in 1931 for the Northern of Portugal Railway, which at that time was also operating the Tamega line of the M.D. Each of the radial wheels was mounted on a Krauss—Helmholz truck, and lateral movement was allowed in the second and fourth coupled axles. The engines had Kylala blast pipes. These were the last steam locomotives built for the metre-gauge, and they were fine machines capable of high speed.

255. 4—6—0T No. E124. Four were built by Borsig in 1908 for the Vale do Vouga Railway. They were pretty little engines and like all the metre-gauge locomotives had vacuum brakes.

256. Four-cylinder compound ▶
0—4—4—0 Mallet tank engine No.
E165. The L.P. cylinders are in
front and attached to the frames
of the Bissel truck. The H.P.
cylinders drive the fixed wheels
and are attached to the main frames.
Twelve engines were built by
Henschel between 1905 and 1908
and there were minor differences
between the batches. They went
to the Minho & Douro lines of the
State Railways.

◀
257. Four-cylinder compound
2—4—6—0 Mallet tank No. E181
with a mixed train from the Corgo
line of the M.D., entering Regua.
Sixteen of these attractive and
successful engines were built for
the M.D. lines of the State Railways
between 1911 and 1923, and two
(including No. E181) for the
Northern of Portugal in 1923.
These latter engines had one side
window in the cab whereas the
M.D. engines had two.

258. Locomotives in the yard of the largest metre-gauge engine shed in Portugal, at the Avenida da Franca in Oporto. In the background is the old Boa Vista terminus, now used for stabling carriages. In the foreground is one of two Mallets built by Henschel for the Tamega Valley line of the M.D.▼

SPANISH NATIONAL RAILWAYS SYSTEM
Red Nacional de los Ferrocarriles Espanoles: R.E.N.F.E.

Gauge: 5ft 5$\frac{15}{16}$ in (1.674m)

The first steam locomotive in Spain was a 2—2—2 with outside cylinders named *Mataro*, one of four built by Jones and Potts of Warrington in 1848. It opened the first railway in Spain, between Barcelona and Mataró, on 5th October, 1848. Railway construction was to the broad gauge from the beginning. Subsequent lines were largely financed by foreign capital, and this influenced the composition of the locomotive stock for many years.

On 1st February, 1941, the Spanish broad gauge railways were nationalised. Unlike Portugal, the organisation included only the broad gauge lines and the many narrow gauge railways were left in private ownership. Some 22 railways formed the R.E.N.F.E., the four major companies being the Northern Railway of Spain (NORTE), the Madrid, Zaragoza and Alicante Railway (M.Z.A.), the Andalusian Railways (ANDALUCES) and the National Western Railway (OESTE), itself an amalgamation of several smaller railways. Another small but important company was the Central of Aragon (C. of A.) which had a number of steam locomotives of great interest.

The Railways of Spain were dreadfully damaged during the Civil War of 1936–39, and although Spain was not a belligerent during the Second War, she was unable to obtain, or to afford, during that time and for long afterwards, the necessary materials to repair and rehabilitate her railway system. Even the identity of much of the locomotive stock was confused, as the opposing sides usually removed works and number plates from engines in territory which they over-ran.

It is frequently said that Spain is a country of contrasts, the old and the new being inextricably mixed up. This was particularly true of locomotives, and it was quite usual to see a steam centenarian working alongside modern electric locomotives and diesel trains. What was, however, most interesting about the steam locomotive in Spain was its infinite variety. Probably only in India was it ever possible to see such a diversity of steam locomotive practice, which included articulated locomotives of the Garratt, Mallet and Kitson Meyer types. There was also an almost infinite variety of components and auxiliaries, as for example Giesl ejectors, Kylchap blast-pipes, poppet valves of several types, feed-water pumps and heaters of almost every known make, many different lubricators, injectors British and German, mechanical stokers, oil-burning apparatus, wet sanding gear, dry sanding gear—the list was almost endless and made Spain a unique centre of interest for the serious student of locomotive practice.

For many years France, Belgium, Britain and Germany were the principal builders of Spanish locomotives, but in later years most were built in Spain by world-famous builders such as La Maquinista and Babcock & Wilcox. As money became available for modernisation, efforts were made to standardise at any rate the larger steam power, though track reconstruction on a vast scale was and still is the greatest need of the R.E.N.F.E.

During the last years of steam, many locomotives were fitted with double blast-pipes and double chimneys, a modification which produced by far the most noteworthy improvements in steaming and fuel economy. There was also a big conversion from coal to oil firing, while other equipment such as roller bearings gave the R.E.N.F.E. a stud of modern and powerful locomotives which required less maintenance and so eased the large demand for manpower which the railways could not properly afford.

For the future, the R.E.N.F.E. is slowly but steadily electrifying its main lines, mostly at 3,000 volts D.C. There is also a considerable mileage of 1,500 volts D.C. electrification, and in some areas it is intended to convert this to 3,000 volts. In the south there is a short length of line operating on 6kV, 25-cycle, three-phase A.C. Diesel locomotives are being introduced for main-line and shunting duties in non-electrified areas and diesel railcars and buses are being increasingly used in suburban and branch-line service. The fastest passenger services in Spain are, and will be, operated by T.A.F. diesel m.-u. trains for second class passengers and by TALGO trains for first class passengers.

▲259. Ex-Norte 0—6—0 No. 030.2077 *La Cañada* leaving Valencia with a *correos* for Villamarchante. Many hundreds of 0—6—0s, some dating from 1857, were at work in the nineteen-sixties. Some had inside cylinders, but this example had outside cylinders with outside Stephenson link motion, and was built by Chemnitz in 1882.

260. Ex-Norte 0—8—0 No. 040.2514. Despite its venerable appearance this locomotive was built as recently as 1909 by Henschel, and was superheated, with piston valves. The valve gear was Walschaert with an eccentric in place of the usual return crank. Spain had many outside-cylinder 0—8—0s of various ages and designs, but none with inside cylinders.▼

261. Ex-Norte 4—6—0 No. 230.2096. Built in Germany and introduced in 1909, this was one of the last series of simple 4—6—0s for the Norte. Sixty were built, with superheaters and piston valves. Earlier series were non-super-heated.

262. Ex-M.Z.A. four-cylinder de Glehn compound 4—6—0 No. 4051 and four-cylinder compound 4—8—0 No. 240.4069 on a troop train at Zaragoza. Despite its French appearance, the 4—6—0 was German-built in 1905 and later engines of the series had piston valves but none were superheated. The 4—8—0 was built by Alco in 1914 and had a common piston valve for each pair of H.P. and L.P. cylinders. ▼

263. 2—6—0 No. 130.2114 was a former Oeste engine originating on one of the constituent companies, the Madrid, Caceres & Portugal. It was a superheated simple engine with piston valves built by Chemnitz in 1909.

264. Ex-M.Z.A. four-cylinder compound 4—6—2 No. 231.4021 with a train for Getafe leaving Madrid (Atocha). Even during what were obviously its last days, this 1913 compound still displayed the hall-marks of the famous Maffei Pacifics with their large L.P. cylinders outside the bar frames and the enormous common piston valve for each H.P./L.P. group. The trailing axle was set well back to the rear of the grate. Two simple Pacifics were built for the M.Z.A. and for the Andaluces, but the only other compound Pacifics were those for the Norte, which were four-cylinder de Glehn compounds built in 1911 and similar in design and appearance to the French Pacifics of that time.

265, 266. Plate 265 (above) shows ex-Norte 2—8—0 No. 140.2263 working freight near Palencia. These 2—8—0s were first built in 1909 and the design remained unchanged until 1941-43, when the last batch was built with O.C. Lentz valves and a higher boiler pressure. Three other railways adopted the same design and the R.E.N.F.E. became the owners of nearly 450 of them. In 1959, one of the later engines with Lentz valves was rebuilt in Vigo with a Crosti boiler of a new type in which the economiser was divided along its axis, gases entering at the top and being exhausted from the bottom part. This enabled a chimney to be used in the conventional position, and a multiple jet blast-pipe was fitted. This engine, No. 140.2438, is shown in **Plate 266** (below).

267. Ex-Norte 2—8—2 No. 141.2007 working freight in Zaragoza. Fifty-two of these typical American-built engines came to the Norte in 1917. They had bar frames and apart from the addition of another sand-box behind the chimney, were little altered during their lives.

268. Oil-burning 2—8—2 No. 141F.2397, with double blast-pipe and chimney and Worthington feed-water pump and heater. This was the modern, general-purpose locomotive introduced on the R.E.N.F.E. in 1953, of which many were built, some by the North British Locomotive Co. The earlier engines had single Kylala blast-pipes and were coal fired. All had plate frames and piston valves, and they were excellent and economical machines. The maximum axle-load was 17.7 *tonnes* and the tractive effort 41,492 pounds.

269. Ex-Oeste 4—8—0 No. 240.2213 with O.C. Lentz valves. The 4—8—0 was a favourite and very numerous type in Spain, the M.Z.A. having the most, including some compounds (Plate 262) and the 1400 class simples, of which 165 were built, including some for Portugal (Plate 247). The Norte had comparatively few 4—8—0s but included in their roster 45 de Glehn compounds.

270. Standard R.E.N.F.E. oil-burning 4—8—0s (No. 240F.2629 in the foreground) waiting to leave Madrid-Atocha shed for the morning expresses. The large group of two-cylinder 4—8—0s with piston valves built for the R.E.N.F.E. originated in 1935 on the Andaluces Ry. and similar engines were bought by both the Oeste and the M.Z.A., before the formation of the R.E.N.F.E. Many were oil-burners and many had double blast-pipes and chimneys. The sloping front to the running plate was characteristic.

271. Ex-Norte four cylinder compound 4—3—2 No. 241.4020 on a freight train near Palencia. The Norte introduced 56 of these German-built engines in 1925, only a few weeks after the C. de F. de l'Est and the P.L.M. had put the first European 4—8—2s into experimental services. Ten further engines were built in Spain for the Norte in 1927 and ten for the Andaluces, who, however, sold them to the Norte. All were de Glehn compounds with four sets of Walschaert gear and independent cut-off, but the four cylinders were in line although the inside L.P. drove the leading coupled axle and the H.P. the second axle. The maximum axle-load was 17.84 *tonnes*.

272. Rebuilt four-cylinder compound 4—8—2 No. 241.4048. In 1939 this engine (originally a standard 4—8—2 as above) was rebuilt on the principles adopted by M. André Chapelon for the P-O Pacifics in France. A double Kylchap blast-pipe was fitted and the cylinders and valves completely redesigned, steam distribution being by Dabeg O.C. poppet valves. The cut-off remained independent. Another five of the older engines were later similarly rebuilt and the design was used for the construction in 1946-7 of 28 new engines for the R.E.N.F.E. The essential dimensions for all the compound 4—8—2s remained the same. ▼

273. Ex-M.Z.A. two-cylinder simple 4—8—2 No. 241.2103 was one of ten engines built by La Maquinista in 1939 which were partly streamlined on the pattern of Gresley's Class A4 Pacifics. They had Dabeg O.C. poppet valves and originally the boiler pressure was 20 Kg/cm³ (284.5 lb/sq in) but was later reduced to 18 Kg/cm³ (256 lb/sq in). The maximum axle-load was $19\frac{1}{4}$ *tonnes* and the tractive effort was 37,217 lb at 65 per cent.

274. Ex-M.Z.A. 4—8—2 No. 241.2078 leaving Tarragona with an express for Valencia. In 1925 the M.Z.A. introduced a two-cylinder simple 4—8—2 very shortly after the début of the Norte engines (Plate 271). During the next 6 years, 95 of these Series 1700 engines were built, mostly with piston valves, but five with O.C. Lentz and 20, like No. 241.2078, with O.C. Dabeg valves and a feed-water pump and heater of the same make. The tractive effort at 65 per cent was 31,900 lb. ▼

275. Oil-burning 4—8—2 No. 241F.2210. The final development of the 4—8—2 in Spain came in 1944 with the introduction of these enormous machines by the R.E.N.F.E. They had two cylinders with O.C. Lentz valves and Kylchap double blast-pipes and chimneys. Provision was made for a trickle of steam to pass through the superheater elements while steam was shut off, to prevent the burning of elements which often occurs in oil-fired locomotives. The large boiler had a combustion chamber and four arch-tubes and was fed by two injectors and an A.C.F.I. pump and heater. T.I.A. water treatment was also provided. The boiler was interchangeable with that of the 2—10—2s (Plate 278) and was nearly identical with that of the 4—8—4s (below). These fine locomotives were used principally on the M.Z.A. main line, which includes long and severe gradients.

276. Oil-burning 4—8—4 No. 242F.2008 on the Iberia express at Vallodolid. The most heavily graded sections of the Irun—Madrid main line are electrified, but between Medina and Avila the gradients are not so severe, and these big express engines were introduced in 1956 to operate fast trains on the non-electrified section. They had roller bearing axle-boxes on all axles and the two cylinders had O.C. Lentz valves. Boilers and fittings were the same as those of the 4—8—2 (above) but the axle-load of 20 *tonnes* was 1 *tonne* less, and the driving wheels had a diameter of 6ft 3in, against the 5ft 8in of the 4—8—2. The small electric light on a stem in front of the chimney enabled the enginemen to see at night the amount and nature of the smoke from the oil-fuel and was fitted to all oil-fired locomotives of the R.E.N.F.E.

277. Ex-C. of A. 0—6—6—0 Mallet compound locomotive No. 060.4004. The Central of Aragon main line between Valencia and Teruel abounds in steep gradients and severe curves and articulated locomotives were used extensively. Garratts largely replaced the Mallets but No. 060.4004 was one of nine engines built by Henschel between 1912 and 1928, which were working in the nineteen-sixties. They had superheaters and piston valves and some were fitted with Westinghouse as well as vacuum brakes. The shapely bell-mouthed chimney was a C. of A. characteristic.

278. Three-cylinder 2—10—2s Nos. 151.3115 and 3116. These huge machines were designed for the Norte but were actually put into service by the R.E.N.F.E. in 1942. They were the heaviest and most powerful 2—10—2s in Europe and their tractive effort (85 per cent) was 72,050 lb. The maximum axle-load was just over 21 *tonnes*, and the radial axle and the leading coupled axle formed a Krauss-Helmholz bogie. The three cylinders were in line, the inside cylinder driving the second and the two outside cylinders the third coupled axles. Steam distribution was by O.C. Lentz valves. All the 20 engines were coal-fired but only two had mechanical stokers. Despite a grate area of 57sq ft, it was within the capabilities of one man to fire these engines on the heavy undulating gradients between Leon and Venta de Baños. ▼

279. Ex-C. of A. oil-burning 4—6—2+2—6—4 Garratt No. 462F.0404 leaving Valencia with an express for Barcelona. In 1931 six of these engines were built under licence by Euskalduna for the Valencia—Teruel line. Very few Garratt locomotives have ever been used in Europe and these were the only European Garratt express locomotives. In their later years, the R.E.N.F.E. converted them to oil firing and used them exclusively on the coast line between Tarragona and Valencia. They had A.C.F.I. feed water equipment and were fitted with both vacuum and Westinghouse air brakes. The large additional sandbox over the leading tank will be noted.

280. Oil-burning 2—8—2+2—8—2 No. 282F.0424. Five freight Garratts were built under licence by Babcock & Wilcox for the C. of A. in 1931. They had the characteristic bell-mouthed chimneys and were coal burners but were later converted for oil fuel. In 1960-61 the same firm built ten new engines to the same design for the R.E.N.F.E. These were oil burners and had stove-pipe chimneys with a second smaller chimney and silencer for the ejector exhaust. There were two Nicholson thermic syphons in the firebox. These were the last steam locomotives to be built for the R.E.N.F.E., and they were able to take 490-*tonne* trains up long gradients of 1 in 47 at 12 m.p.h. ▼

281. 0—8—0T No. 040.0231 *Gallarta*. This was typical of the many numerically small classes of diverse locomotives owned by the smaller constituent companies which were absorbed by the R.E.N.F.E. Two of these engines were built by Krauss in 1910 for the F.C. de Triano and were used by the R.E.N.F.E. for shunting at Bilbao.

282. Ex-Norte four cylinder de Glehn compound 4—8—4T No. 242.0406. Built by the Sté. Alsacienne in 1913, the French inspiration in this design is unmistakable, although it preceded the P.L.M. 4—8—4T by 14 years.

283. Ex-M.Z.A. 4—8—4T No. 242.0255. There were three batches of these engines built between 1924 and 1927 and having different tank capacities. They were all fine-looking machines and, with 60 engines, formed by far the largest and most important group of main-line tank engines in Spain.

SWEDISH STATE RAILWAYS

Statens Jarnvagar: S.J.

Gauge : 4ft 8½in (1.435m) and narrow gauges

The first steam locomotive in Sweden was an 0—4—0 named *Forstlingen* built in 1847 for the Norberg Railway by Munktells Mechanical Works, Eskilstuna. The gauge was 3 Swedish feet (2ft 11$\frac{9}{32}$in). The engine had two outside cylinders placed between the axles, with connecting rods from each end of the piston rods to drive each pair of wheels, which were also coupled. It was unsatisfactory and was later altered completely and converted to standard gauge.

The first railways in Sweden were privately built and were narrow gauge lines, the first standard gauge railways being completed in 1856. In 1855 construction of the Swedish State Railways began, and from then on, both private and state lines were built. From 1879 the State Railways have absorbed many private lines but not all, and now the S.J. owns and operates about 90 per cent of the route mileage in Sweden, most of it electrified. The S.J. also operates a considerable narrow-gauge mileage, mostly of 891 mm gauge.

The standard gauge steam locomotives of the S.J. were of many different types, as a result of so many of them having been taken over from private companies who favoured inside cylinders and had numerous classes of light 2—6—0s, 4—6—0s and 0—8—0s, most of which came into the S.J. at one time or another. None were of outstanding design, though they were quite characteristic. All locomotives in Sweden were built by outside firms and none by any of the companies or by the S.J. Like most European countries Sweden bought some standard Prussian locomotives, notably the G-8/1 0—8—0s which became S.J. Class G, and in 1954 two British Austerity 2—8—0s (Plate 175) were purchased from the Netherlands Railways and became S.J. Class G–11. The cabs were enclosed and the tenders reconstructed to the three-axle type in order to get them on to existing turntables.

The heaviest traffic in Sweden is carried by the iron-ore line from Kiruna to the Norwegian frontier and on to Narvik. This line was completely electrified by 1923 but before that, several heavy freight engine classes were used, notably some large 0—10—0s built in 1909 (Plate 290). Apart from eleven Fairlie locomotives of the 1870s, none of the standard gauge railways used articulated locomotives, but some Mallets were used on the narrow gauge lines.

After 1920, most of the heavy passenger and freight locomotives were three-cylinder simples, though Sweden has only ever had one class of four-cylinder simples—some 4—6—0s of 1917, built for a private line, which later became S.J. Class B–4. Three series of four-cylinder compounds were built, the most important of which were the S.J. Pacifics of Class F, introduced in 1914 and sold to Denmark in 1937 to become D.S.B. Class E (Plate 54). The last tender locomotives to be built for the S.J. were ten three-cylinder 4—8—0s of Class E–10 in 1947 for freight duties, and the last tank locomotives were twenty 2—6—4T Class S–1 put into service in 1952 (Plates 291 and 292).

The most important remaining private railway is the T.G.O.J. (the Grangesberg–Oxelosund Railway), which is now electrified but which still keeps in store three Ljungstrom non-condensing turbine locomotives. In 1957 this company sold to the S.J. five 0—8—0s, which were the first three-cylinder engines in Sweden (1913) and which became S.J. Class E–12. Several 2—6—2Ts were also sold at this time (S.J. Class S–13) and were the last steam engines purchased by the S.J.

The number of locomotives in Sweden is a military secret and it is probable that a number of steam locomotives will be kept in store in forest and mountain hide-outs, long after the last days of steam. It is also probable that many classes officially extinct are among those stored against a national emergency.

Railway electrification first started in 1895 between Stockholm and Djursholm, but it was twenty years before any great progress was made. Now more than 50 per cent of the standard gauge lines are electrified using 15 kV single-phase A.C., with a frequency of 16$\frac{2}{3}$ cycles. Diesel hydro-mechanical railcars are widely used for passenger services on secondary lines and the S.J. has an assortment of diesel locomotives with hydraulic and electric transmissions. This will be the pattern of Swedish railways for the future.

284. Former Stockholm-Westeras-Bergslagens Railway (S.W.B.) 4—6—0 No. 1696 Class B with a fast train from Borlange to Mora. Forming the most numerous S.J. passenger class, these engines were obviously inspired by K.P.E.V. Clasa P-8 (Plate 118). Ninety-six were built 1909-19 for S.J. and three for S.W.B. in 1943-4. All had bar frames and the maximum axle-load was 15.9 tonnes. S.W.B. engines had roller bearing axle-boxes. larger superheaters and more heating surface than the S.J. engines.

285. 4—6—0 No 1687 S.J. Class A-7. Introduced in 1910 by the Bergslagernas Railway, (B.J.) this became the most important passenger class for the private railways, several of which adopted the design. The engines had plate frames and the axle-load was only 13.1 tonnes. B.J. engines had Deeley valve gear but those for other railways had Walschaerts gear, some with inside eccentrics and others with outside return cranks. ▼

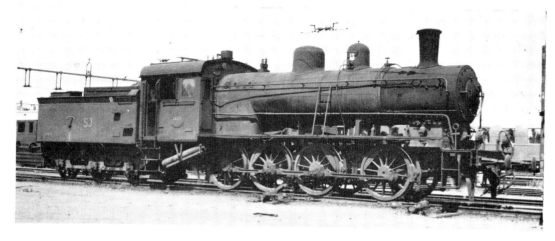

286. 0—8—0 No. 1460 Class E. These light-weight superheater freight engines were built for S.J. from 1907-20 and were the most numerous of any class in Sweden. They had a short wheel-base and the axle load was only 12.5 tonnes. Many of them were rebuilt with a leading radial truck and classified E-2 (Plate 288).

287. 0—8—0 No. 1824 S.J. Class E-4. This was one of a number of small 0—8—0s similar to S.J. Class E (Plate 286) built originally in 1907 for the Bergslagernas Railway (B.J.) as their Class N-3. The Boras-Alvesta and the Halsingborg - Hassleholm Railways also had engines of this class.

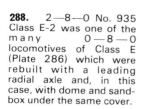

288. 2—8—0 No. 935 Class E-2 was one of the many 0—8—0 locomotives of Class E (Plate 286) which were rebuilt with a leading radial axle and, in this case, with dome and sandbox under the same cover.

289. 4—6—0 No. 1510 Class A-3 was one of two engines built for the Ostkustbanen (O.K.B.) in 1928 as the Class H. The design was developed from that of the Class A-7 seen in Plate 285. Of interest were the outside bogie frames and the compensating beams and the German-type smoke deflectors. The valve gear was Walschaerts with outside return cranks on the leading outside crank pins. The boilers were from S.J. rebuilt Atlantics which were purchased by O.K.B.

290. 0—10—0 No. 977, Class R. These powerful engines were built in 1909 for the Kiruna ore traffic of the State Railways. After the electrification of this Arctic Circle line, the Class R went south to work mineral traffic between Falun and Gavle. They had bar frames and the maximum axle-load was 17 *tonnes*; the tractive effort was 41,360 lb. Note the ash-chute in front of the smokebox. In the early 'sixties, it was strange to see on the cylinder cover a plate inscribed—OFVERHETTARE W. SCHMIDT. PATENT No. 904. 1909.

146

▲ **291.** Three-cylinder 4—8—0 No. 1739, Class E-10. Ten of these engines were built by Nydquist & Holm in 1947 and were the last tender engines to be built for the S.J. Steam distribution was by three sets of Walschaert gear, and the inside cylinder drove the leading coupled axle. The maximum axle-load was only 12.8 *tonnes* and the tractive effort was 26,620 lb. The semi-cylindrical tender tank was first introduced for the four-cylinder compound Pacifics in 1914.

292. 2—6—4T No. 1910, Class S-1. Twenty of these neat little engines were built in 1953 and were not only the last tank engines, but the last steam engines to be built for the S.J. The maximum driving axle-load was 12.6 *tonnes*, but the carrying axle-load was 14.0 *tonnes*. ▼

293. 0—8—0T No. 1130, Class N. Two batches were built, non-superheater, 20 in 1900-01 and 44 in 1912-20, of which No. 1130 is one. They had Helmholtz valve gear and when later superheated, retained their balanced slide valves. They were the first engines in Sweden to have totally enclosed cabs.

294. 2—6—2T No. 1881, Class S-7. This little superheater tank engine was built for the Bergslagarnas Railway in 1924. The acetylene gas bottle for the headlights can be seen below the smokebox.

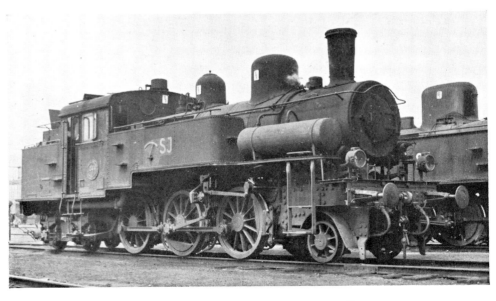

295. 2—6—4T No. 1344, Class J These odd-looking inside-cylinder mixed-traffic engines were introduced on the S.J. in 1914. The return crank and expansion link for the Walschaert gear were outside. The maximum axle-load was only 11.0 *tonnes* and the trailing truck had outside frames.

SWISS FEDERAL RAILWAYS

Schweizerische Bundesbahnen: S.B.B.

Chemins de Fer Federaux Suisses: C.F.F.

Gauges : 4ft 8½in (1.435m)

3ft 3⅜in (1.0m)

The first railway in Switzerland, opened in 1844, was a French-operated line between Strasbourg and Bâle which between St. Louis and Bâle, about 1½ miles, ran in Swiss territory. The first locomotives to run in Switzerland were, therefore, French and particulars of them are not in existence. The first Swiss railway proper was between Baden and Zurich, and the first Swiss steam locomotive was an outside cylinder 4—2—0 named *Limmat*, built by the Kessler Works at Carlsrühe in 1847 under the supervision of Nicolas Riggenbach.

The Swiss Federal Railways were formed by an amalgamation in 1902 of the five largest private railways and their associated companies. They now operate about 80 per cent of the standard gauge lines but only 46 miles of metre gauge. All the S.B.B. lines are electrified using alternating single-phase current at 15 kV, 16⅔ cycles, generated by water power. Seventy diesel locomotives are used for some shunting duties. The majority of the numerous privately owned railways are also electrified, but several use diesel traction and keep a few steam locomotives (mostly rack and narrow gauge) in reserve.

It is interesting that, despite the mountainous nature of the country and a number of long and severe gradients, the Swiss Railways never owned any big steam power, and the most powerful locomotives were four-cylinder compound 2—10—os (Plate 297) which lasted until the end of steam. For passenger duties several series of four-cylinder compound 4—6—os sufficed, and a large proportion of steam power consisted of 2—6—2Ts. During the twenties, the S.B.B. experimented with condensing turbine locomotives and later with a 2—6—2T with a very high pressure boiler, but as in other countries, the ideas were found impracticable. Articulated locomotives were confined to one series of 0—4—4—0 Mallet tender engines and three series of similar tank engines owned by the constituent companies before the turn of the century.

Generally speaking, then, Swiss steam locomotives were outstanding neither in interest nor in design, though one extraordinary conversion deserves mention. During the Second War, coal was almost unobtainable in Switzerland and in 1942 two standard 0—6—0Ts of Series E3/3 were equipped to use electric "firing" to raise steam. Pantographs were fitted on top of the cabs to collect the necessary current for these electric-steam locomotives.

The classification of Swiss steam locomotives was in two parts, first a capital letter from A to D for tender engines and a capital E followed by a small letter for tank engines. These letters indicated maximum permissible speeds, thus:—

Series A tender engines: maximum speed over 75 km/hr

  ,,   Ea tank engines & Series B tender engines : maximum speed 75 km/hr

  ,,   Eb ,,   ,,   ,,   ,,   C   ,,   ,, :   ,,   ,, 65 km/hr

  ,,   Ec ,,   ,,   ,,   ,,   D   ,,   ,, :   ,,   ,, 55 km/hr

  ,,   E   ,,   ,, were for shunting.

The second part of the classification showed the number of coupled axles and the total number of axles. Thus Series A 3/5 was a tender engine which could travel at more than 75 km/hr and had five axles, of which three were coupled, *i.e.*, a 4—6—0. Series Ec 3/5 was a tank engine which could travel up to 55 km/hr and which also had five axles, three of them coupled, and was a 2—6—2T. The description 3/5 fits equally well the types 4—6—0, 0—6—4, 2—6—2, but was more definite on the S.B.B. in that there were no 0—6—4 or 2—6—2 tender engines and no 4—6—0 or 0—6—4 tank engines. A further example is Series E 4/4 which describes a shunting tank engine with four axles, all of them coupled, *i.e.*, an 0—8—0T. Similar methods of locomotive classification by axles are to be found elsewhere, for example on the Turkish State Railways (*q.v.*)

The future motive power of the S.B.B. is electric with some diesel shunters, as already described.

▲ **296.** Four-cylinder compound 4—6—0 No. 760, Series A3/5. These de Glehn compounds were first built for the Jura Simplon Railway in 1902 and for the S.B.B. until 1907. They were not superheated, and the tractive effort was 21,243 lb. The H.P. cylinders were outside and the valves were driven by Walschaert gear. Joy gear was used for the inside L.P. valves, the cut-off being independent for each group. Other series of compound 4—6—0s had outside L.P. cylinders and were superheated; some of these were sold to Holland in 1946 and ended their days on the N.S. The Gothard Railway's four-cylinder compound 4—6—0s were of the well known Maffei type with a common piston valve for each pair of H.P./L.P. cylinders, and there were similar 2—8—0s for freight traffic.

297. Four-cylinder compound 2—10—0 No. 2972, Series C5/6, with a freight train at Buchs. Twenty-eight of these engines and two with four high-pressure cylinders were built between 1913 and 1917 and they remained the most powerful steam locomotives in Switzerland. The compounds had a tractive effort of 44,939 lb and a maximum axle-load of 15.3 *tonnes*. The L.P. cylinders were outside and the H.P. inside, each with its own piston valve, and the cut-off was independent. The Series C5/6 were popular machines which did their best work on the Gothard line. During the First War, a number of them, with their crews, were loaned to the P.L.M. Railway in France. ▼

298. 2—6—2T No. 5881, Series Eb3/5. Nine of these handsome engines were built by Maffei in 1910 for the Toggenbourg-Lac de Constance Railway, and they originally had Clench steam driers. When this railway was electrified in 1931/2, these engines were sold to the S.B.B., who replaced the steam driers by Schmidt superheaters. A mirror was fitted in the cab to enable the driver to see the gauges when the engine was running bunker-first.

299. 0—8—0T No. 8917, Series E4/4 (rebuild) shunting at Buchs. There were nine of these superheater tank engines, which were 1930-33 rebuilds of two-cylinder simple 2—8—0s of Series C4/5. They had steam reversers.

300. 0—6—0WT No. 8470, Series E3/3. The S.B.B. had 83 of these shunting tanks, which were developed by the Swiss Locomotive Company. Similar engines were to be found in other European countries, notably Norway.

301. 2—6—0T No. 6512, Series Ec3/4, was one of 11 engines built by the Swiss Locomotive Company in 1900 for the Jura-Simplon Railway. Two were superheated.

302. 2—6—2T No. 5819, Series Eb3/5. This was one of 34 superheater passenger tanks built for the S.B.B. between 1911 and 1916 for local passenger, suburban and banking duties on the shorter inclines.

TURKISH STATE RAILWAYS
Turkiye Cumhuriyeti Devlet Demiryollari Isletmesi: T.C.D.D.

Gauge : 4ft 8½in (1.435m)

Also 77 miles of 5ft 0in (1.524m) gauge from Sarikamis connecting with the Russian Railways at Hudut, and 75 miles of 2ft 5½in (0.750m) gauge lines, partly rack operated, connecting the 5ft 0in and the standard gauge lines.

The first railway in Turkey was the British owned and built Ottoman Railway from Smyrna (now Izmir) to Aidin, opened in 1860.

The first locomotives in Turkey were ten outside-cylinder 4—4—0s built by Robert Stephenson & Co. in 1859. No. 1 hauled the inaugural train. These engines were later given new boilers and they remained in service until the 1930s.

The T.C.D.D. was formed in 1927 by the nationalisation of the Anatolian & Baghdad Railways and during the next nine years all the independent companies were brought in, the last being the first railway in Turkey, the Ottoman Railway.

The main line in European Turkey connects Istanbul with Greece and Bulgaria, but traffic is light compared with that of the lines in Asia.

The steam locomotive in Turkey reflected the competing interests of three great powers: most of the older locomotives were of British design and construction, a few were built in France, but by far the greatest number of the later designs were German, though not all were built in Germany.

Locomotives could be divided into three groups :

(i) those having a maximum axle-load of up to 21 *tonnes* and used on the heavily-laid main lines in Asia, as for example Haydarpasa–Ankara–Sivas.

(ii) those having an axle load of up to 17 *tonnes* for service on the European main line and on the lines of the former Ottoman Railway.

(iii) those having an axle load not exceeding 13.5 *tonnes* for the many lightly-laid routes, particularly in western and southern Turkey, as, for example, the important line between Izmir and Afyon of the former Smyrna, Cassaba and Extensions Railway.

By far the most widely used locomotive type in Turkey was the 2—10—0 and several series were built with axle-loads ranging from 20.2 *tonnes* to 13.5 *tonnes*. After the Second War, the T.C.D.D. received 53 German Kriegsloks of Type 52 (Plate 312) which were popular and useful machines. On the other hand the 48 three-cylinder engines (150.X.) bought from the S.N.C.F. in the late '50s (Plate 304) were never liked in Turkey. The most important locomotives were the big two-cylinder 2—10—0s (Plate 305) first built by Henschel in 1937 and of which successive batches were built in Britain (1948) and Czechoslovakia (1949) and finally two by the Works at Sivas and Eskisehir in 1961. These were the first and only steam locomotives of Turkish construction and they reflected great credit on their builders who, always short of money and equipment, laboured under great difficulty.

As a result of the First War, the T.C.D.D. inherited a number of standard Prussian types, while after the Second War, Stanier 2—8—0s, U.S. Army 2—8—0s and Baldwin 2—8—2s built for the Ministry of Supply (Plate 310), were used for many years, as well as the German 52s already mentioned. Some very large and heavy 2—10—0s were also purchased from the Vulcan Iron Works of America (Plate 306).

With very little money available for new stock, the T.C.D.D. had to make do with many different types and classes of locomotives purchased, sometimes second-hand, wherever terms were favourable. Often spare parts were a constant headache for the engineers trying to maintain these many types and great ingenuity was shown in the works by making new parts out of scanty materials. Also as a result of the different policies adopted by the constituent companies of the T.C.D.D., brakes were of several types and resulted in all rolling stock having to be dual-fitted. Steam brakes, vacuum brakes and three types of air brakes (Westinghouse, Knor and Kuntze-Knor) were in common use.

The classification of Turkish steam locomotives was contained in the five-digit number—the first two digits of which indicated first the number of coupled axles and second, the total number of axles. The last three digits were the running number of the engine; in tank engines four digits only were used, the last two being the running number. Thus engine 56116 was a 2—10—0 No. 116 and 3710 was a 4—6—4T No. 10.

The future motive power in Turkey on the main line from Haydarpasa to Ankara is to be electric using 50-cycle monophase A.C. (the Istanbul-Halkali suburban line in European Turkey already operates on this system); diesel-electric locomotives and diesel-hydraulic railcars will operate all other services.

▲ **303.** 2—8—2 No. 46057. The picture shows the engine being hosed down with hot water from its own injector. Eleven of these engines were built by Henschel in 1927 for the heavy express trains between Haydarpasa and Ankara, and they were the only express locomotives ever to be built for the T.C.D.D. The driving wheels were 5ft 8¾in diameter and the leading pair formed a Krauss truck with the leading radial wheels. They were magnificent machines—free steaming and free running and they were allowed to travel at up to 100 Km/hr (62½ m.p.h.)—the highest limit for steam.

304. Three-cylinder 2—10—0 No. 56747 was one of 48 S.N.C.F. engines of Series 150.X. (German Type 44) sold to Turkey in 1958 (Page 41 and Plate 114). Behind is a U.S. Army 2—8—0 built to British loading gauge restrictions (Plate 160). Fifty-three went to Turkey after the Second War, and they were converted to burn oil. ▼

305. 2—10—0 No. 56141. These were the standard heavy mixed-traffic engines of the T.C.D.D. and there were 168 of them built in batches by Henschel (1937), Vulcan Foundry (1948) and Skoda (1949). Two further engines were built by the railway works in Turkey in 1961. There were detail differences between batches; those built by Skoda (of which No. 56141 is one) had the heaviest axleload but were always considered to embody the best workmanship. All these 2—10—0s had bar frames and Riggenbach counter-pressure braking. Some were oil-fired though most were hand-fired coal-burners. The leading coupled wheels formed a Krauss truck with the radial wheels, and these and the second pair of coupled wheels formed a compensated suspension unit, the last three pairs of wheels forming another such unit. Their maximum permitted speed was 70 Km/hr (47¼ m.p.h.).

306. 2—10—0 No. 56341. This was one of 88 stoker-fired engines built by the Vulcan Iron Works of America in 1948. They were considerably heavier than the European-built 2—10—0s and had cast-steel engine beds with frames, smokebox saddle and cylinders in an integral casting. Considerable modifications were made to them by the T.C.D.D., including alteration of the weight distribution and springing.

307. 4—8—0 No. 46016. Twenty-five 4—8—0s were built in two batches, by Henschel in 1926 and by Henschel and Krupp in 1934. They were ponderous machines with plate frames and had many parts standard with the Prussian 0—10—0 of Class G-10 and the 4—6—4T of Class T-18. They were hand-fired coal-burners and some of them finished their days working the Haydarpasa suburban service—tender-first in one direction.

308. 2—8—0 No. 45025 with a south-bound freight at Eskisehir. These engines were introduced in 1929 and they were very similar to the Prussian Class G-8/2. Sixty-two were built in Belgium by Tubize and in Sweden by Nohab, and they had larger cylinders and different boiler dimensions from their German prototypes, though they were classed on the T.C.D.D. as G-8/2.

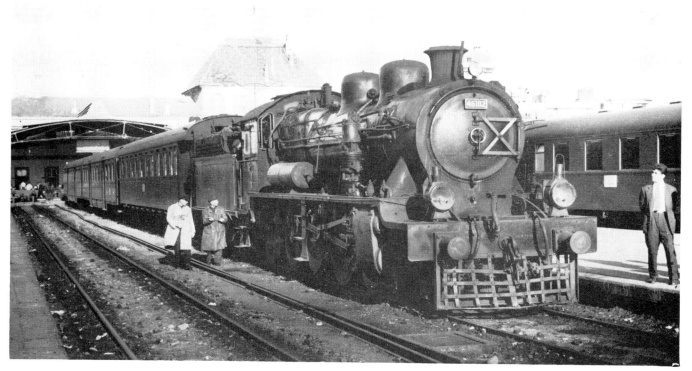

309. 2—8—2 No. 46102 with the Ege (Aegean) Express about to leave Izmir (Basmahane) for Ankara. The train was steam-hauled only to Balikesir, 151 miles. Six of these handsome engines were built by Robert Stephenson in 1929 for the Ottoman Railway. They had plate frames and a maximum axle-load of only 11.9 *tonnes*. The tractive effort was 23,042 lb. Weir feed-water pumps and heaters were fitted.

310. 2—8—2 No. 46203 on a suburban train leaving Ankara. The Turkish Railways received 53 of these Baldwin-built, Ministry of Supply locomotives, the first in 1942. They were rugged machines with bar frames and on the Ankara suburban trains they ran tender-first in one direction as there are no turntables at suburban termini in Turkey.

▲311. 2—10—0 No. 56911 and 0—8—0 No. 44064 leaving Izmir with a freight for Ankara via the Cassaba line. The former Ottoman Railway works at Halkapinar are in the background. The two-cylinder 2—10—0s Nos. 56911-18 were built for the French operated Smyrna, Cassaba & Extensions Railway by Corpet Louvert in 1927. Their maximum axle-load was 13.5 *tonnes*. The Prussian G-8 was one of ten built for the S.C. & E. by Linke-Hoffman in 1924. They had smaller boilers than the later Class G-8/1 (Plate 46), the grate area being 2.35m² (25sq ft) and the working pressure 12 Kg/cm² (171 lb/sq in). The maximum axle-load was 14.4 *tonnes*.

312. Bandirma train at the Basmahane station (ex-S.C. & E. Ry.) Izmir. 2—10—0 No. 56553, the last of the 53 German Kriegsloks of Type 52 (Plate 218) to come to Turkey and classified K-52 on the T.C.D.D. With bar frames and a maximum axle-load of only 15.3 *tonnes*, these were ideal engines for the lightly laid tracks of western Turkey. They were also used on the European lines of the T.C.D.D. ▼

▲313. 2—6—0 No. 34003 with intermediate carrying axle between the second and third coupled axles. Borsig built a series of 2—6—0s for the Baghdad Railway in 1910 and they proved so satisfactory that nine similar engines were ordered from the same builders in 1911 for the Anatolian Railway. However, the 44 *tonnes* on the coupled axles of the Bagdad engines was too heavy for the track of the Anatolian Railway, so by introducing a carrying axle, the adhesive weight was reduced to 41.5 *tonnes*, though the total weight of the engine was, of course, increased. This principle was adopted only in two other known cases, both 0—6—0Ts, first for the Nord Railway of France and the second for 10 Belpaire engines of the Belgian Railway in 1873. The extra carrying wheels were, in all cases, flangeless, and the Turkish engines were always officially described as 1C (2—6—0).

314. 2—8—0 No. 45509 Eighteen of these light 2—8—0s were built by Batignolles in 1925. They were used on the European lines and had A.C.F.I. feed pumps and heaters. The axle-load was 13.5 *tonnes*.

315. 2—10—2 No. 57016. Twenty-seven of these engines were built by Henschel and by Krupp in 1932 for freight and heavy passenger service on the lightly laid tracks of western Turkey. The maximum axle-load was only 13.5 *tonnes* and the tractive effort 41,760 lb. The boilers were identical with those of the 4—8—0s (Plate 307) and like them, the 2—10—2s had plate frames. Cylinders, valve gear and many other parts were standard with the Prussian 0—10—0s of Class G-10 (Plate 215) of which the Turks had 49.

316. Three-cylinder 2—10—2T No. 5703 was one of four engines, built by Henschel in 1952 for banking on the 10 miles of steep gradients (1 in 29—1 in 40) between Bilecik and Karakuyu on the Haydarpasa—Ankara main line. Although the design was similar to the German Type 85, cylinder and boiler dimensions were different and the working pressure was higher.

317. 2—6—2T No. 3554 with Ottoman line suburban train from Izmir (Alsancak) to Seydikoy crossing the Smyrna, Cassaba & Extensions line on the level at Hilal. Ten of these 2—6—2Ts were built by Maffei in 1911 for the Istanbul—Halkali service in Europe, and they were sent to Izmir when that line was electrified.

318. 4—6—4T No. 3704 on a Haydarpasa suburban train. Eight of these engines were built for Turkey by Henschel in 1925 to the designs of the Prussian Class T-18.

319. 0—4—0 square saddle tank No. 2204. Several of these engines were built by Sharp Stewart in 1889 for the Ottoman Railway and they spent most of their time shunting the docks at Izmir. During the last days of steam, they were the oldest engines at work on the T.C.D.D.

320. 0—6—0 side and well tank No. 3354. Built by Maffei in 1912 this was typical of several classes of shunting tank engines taken over by the T.C.D.D. from the original companies.

321. 0—8—2T No. 4503. With its British ancestry never in doubt, this engine was one of three built for the Ottoman Railway in 1911 by Robert Stephenson, who also built four 0—8—0 tender engines of similar appearance and dimensions for the same company. Behind the chimney can be seen the vacuum brake ejector exhaust pipe.

TABLES OF DIMENSIONS
Headings

Column No.

1   PLATE Number in book.

2   Identity of locomotive—type, class, group, etc.

3   DIAMETER of DRIVING WHEELS in *inches* to one decimal place on top line, in *millimetres* on lower line.

4   CYLINDERS, NUMBER AND DIAMETER in *inches* to two decimal places on top line, in *millimetres* on lower line. All dimensions refer to two-cylinder simple locomotives unless noted otherwise thus:—

         (3) indicates 3-cylinder simple.

         (4)   ,,   4-   ,,   ,,

         XXXX/yyyy indicates 1 H.P. and 1 L.P. i.e., two-cylinder compound.

         XXXX/(2)yyyy   ,,   1 H.P. and 2 L.P. i.e., three-cylinder compound.

         (2) XXXX/(2)yyyy   ,,   2 H.P. and 2 L.P. i.e., four-cylinder compound.

5   CYLINDERS, STROKE in *inches* to two decimal places on top line, in *millimetres* on lower line. When the stroke varies with the diameter in compound locomotives, two corresponding figures are given separated by an oblique.

6   BOILER PRESSURE in *pounds per square inch*, to nearest pound, on top line, in *Kilogrammes per square centimetre* to nearest half kilogramme on lower line. (1 Kg/cm² = 14.22 lb/sq. in).

7   GRATE AREA in *square feet* to nearest square foot, on top line, in *square metres*, to one or two decimal places on lower line.

8   REMARKS column. All locomotives are superheated, unless indicated by N.S. (not superheated) in this column. Tractive Effort, where given, is calculated at 85 per cent of boiler pressure unless stated otherwise.

Conversion Tables

In many cases the exact conversions from millimetres to inches and vice versa run to many places of decimals. Therefore in these tables there are several slight discrepancies, for example, a cylinder stroke of 660 mm. in a continental built engine is given as 25.98 in. In British and American built engines having a stroke of 26 in., the metric equivalent is also given as 660 mm.

Continuous Brakes

Most European countries adopted the air brake as standard, but on some railways, notably those of Austria and Denmark, the automatic vacuum brake was in general use until the nineteen-forties when, under the impetus of German occupation, the railways of both these countries began the change-over to air brakes. In Britain a number of pre-grouping railways used air brakes but a decision was made after the grouping in 1923 to adopt the vacuum brake as standard. In Turkey both types of brake are still in common use, though air brakes are used in all new construction and the number of dual fitted locomotives and rolling stock units is being thereby reduced. The vacuum brake now remains as standard only on the railways of Spain, Portugal and Great Britain.

AUSTRIA. O.B.B.

1	2	3	4	5	6	7	8
	2—2—0 AUSTRIA	60 1524	10 254	14 356	50 3.5	— —	N.S.
1	2—8—0 156	49.5 1258	22.44 570	24.88 632	185 13	42 3.9	
2	2—6—2 135	61.9 1574	18.70/27.16 475/690	28.34 720	213 15	33 3.0	
3	2—6—2 35	61.9 1574	18.70 475	28.34 720	213 15	33 3.0	
4	4—6—0 38	66.9 1700	21.65 550	25.98 660	185 13	39 3.6	
5	4—8—0 33	66.9 1700	22.04 560	28.34 720	213 15	49 4.5	
6	2—8—4 12	74.8 1900	25.59 650	28.34 720	213 15	51 4.7	
7	0—10—0 157	49.5 1258	23.22/33.46 590/850	24.88 632	199 14	37 3.4	
8	2—10—0 258	55.5 1410	24.01 610	28.34 720	199 14	48 4.4	
11	2—2—2T 69	55.5 1410	13.58 345	18.89 480	156 11	11 1.0	N.S.
12	2—4—2T 3071	55.5 1410	11.42 290	22.44 570	228 16	9 0.8	
13	2—6—0T 91	43.3 1100	14.56/22.44 370/570	22.44 570	185 13	15 1.4	N.S.
14	4—6—2T 77	61.9 1574	18.70 475	28.34 720	185 13	29 2.7	
15	4—6—4T 78	61.9 1574	19.68 500	28.34 720	185 13	39 3.6	
16	2—10—2T 95	49.5 1258	23.22 590	24.88 632	199 14	37 3.4	
17	2—8—2T 93	43.3 1100	17.71 450	22.44 570	199 14	22 2.0	
18	0—8—0T 392	43.3 1100	20.86 530	22.44 570	199 14	22 2.0	

AUSTRIA. O.B.B.

RACK AND ADHESION LOCOMOTIVES

1	2	3	4	5	6	7	8	
19	0—6—2T 97	40.5 1030	(2)18.89:(2)16.53 (2)480:(2)420	(2)19.68:(2)17.71 (2)500:(2)450	156 11	24 2.2	N.S.	⎫ ⎬ Not compound. ⎪ Abt rack system. ⎬ Rack wheels in ⎪ all engines are ⎭ 688mm (27.1in) diam.
20	0—12—0T 197	40.5 1030	(2)22.44:(2)16.53 (2)570:(2)420	(2)20.47:(2)17.71 (2)520:(2)450	185 13	36 3.3	N.S.	
21/22	2—12—2T 297	40.5 1030	(2)24.01:(2)15.75 (2)610:(2)400	(2)20.47:(2)19.68 (2)520:(2)500	228 16	42 3.9	—	

AUSTRIA. G.K.B.

1	2	3	4	5	6	7	8
23	0—6—0 29	50.6 1285	18.11 460	24.88 632	128 9	17 1.59	N.S.
24	4—4—0 17C	68.5 1740	16.73 425	23.62 600	171 12	25 2.3	N.S.
25	2—8—0 170	51.1 1298	21.26/31.49 540/800	24.88 632	185 13	42 3.9	N.S.
26	0—6—0T 32d–1	38.6 980	12.20 310	18.89 480	171 12	11 1.0	N.S.
27	2—6—2T 30	51.1 1298	20.47/29.13 520/740	24.88 632	185 13	23 2.1	N.S.

For locomotives of German prototypes, see GERMANY (pages 168–169).

BELGIUM. S.N.C.B.

1	2	3	4	5	6	7	8
	L'ELEPHANT 0—4—2	54 1372	14 356	18 457	—	—	N.S.
	LA FLECHE 2—2—2	60 1524	11 280	18 457	—	—	N.S.
28	4—6—2 10	77.9 1980	(4)19.68 (4)500	25.98 660	199 14	54 4.9	Grate area 49.3 sq.ft. in later engines
29	4—6—2 1	77.9 1980	(4)16.53 (4)420	28.34 720	256 18	54 4.9	
30	4—4—2 12	82.7 2100	18.89 480	28.34 720	256 18	40 3.7	
31	4—6—0 40	61.9 1575	19.01 483	25.98 660	190 13.3	—	
32	4—6—0 7	70.9 1800	(2)15.74/(2)23.62 (2)400/(2)600	25.19 640	228 16	33 3.08	
35	2—8—0 31	59.8 1520	22.44 570	28.00 711	199 14	35 3.25	
36	2—8—0 38	59.8 1520	24.00 610	28.00 711	199 14	40 3.7	
37	2—8—0 29	60.4 1524	22.00 559	28.00 711	228 16	48 4.4	
38	0—6—0 41	59.8 1520	19.68 500	25.98 660	192 13.5	27 2.5	
39	4—4—2T 15	70.9 1800	17.32 440	24.00 610	178 12.5	27 2.5	N.S. B.P. orig. 156 lb/sq.in.
40	0—6—0PT 51	47.2 1200	14.96 380	18.11 460	121 8.5	17 1.5	N.S.
41	0—6—0T 58	48.0 1219	16.00 406	24.00 610	190 13.3	—	N.S.
42	0—8—0T 53	49.7 1262	18.89 480	23.62 600	178 12.5	24 2.2	N.S.
43	2—6—2ST 57	44.0 1118	17.00 432	24.00 610	180 12.65	—	

For locomotives of German prototypes see GERMANY (pages 168–169).

DENMARK. D.S.B.

1		3	4	5	6	7	8
	ODIN 2—2—2	60 1524	15 381	20 508	70 4.9	— —	N.S.
48	4—4—0 C	73.5 1866	16.92 430	24.01 610	171 12	20 1.8	
49	4—4—0 K-2	73.5 1866	16.92 430	24.01 610	171 12	20 1.8	
50	4—4—2 P-1	78.1 1984	(2)13.38/(2)22.44 (2)340/(2)570	23.62 600	213 15	35 3.23	
51	4—6—2 PR	68.1 1730	(2)14.17/(2)23.62 (2)360/(2)600	25.19 640	185 13	28 2.6	
52	2—6—0 D-2	55.2 1404	18.11 460	24.01 610	171 12	20 1.8	
53	4—6—0 R-11	73.5 1866	(3)18.50 (3)470	26.37 670	171 12	28 2.6	
54/ 55	4—6—2 E	74.6 1896	(2)16.53/(2)24.80 (2)420/(2)630	25.98 660	185 13	39 3.6	
56/ 57	2—8—0 H	55.2 1404	(3)18.50 (3)470	26.37 670	171 12	28 2.6	
58	0—6—0T F	49.3 1252	16.0 406	22.04 560	171 12	11 1.0	N.S.
59	0—8—0T Q	49.3 1252	18.11 460	24.01 610	171 12	20 1.8	
60	2—6—4T S	68.1 1730	(3)16.92 (3)430	26.37 670	171 12	26 2.4	

FINLAND. V.R.

1	2	3	4	5	6	7	8
	ILMARINEN 4—4—0	60 1524	15.98 406	20.04 509	114 8	— —	N.S.
61	Hv-4	62.0 1575	17.71 450	24.01 610	171 12	16 1.45	
62	Hv-2	68.9 1750	20.07 510	23.62 600	171 12	21 1.96	
63/ 64	Hr-1	74.8 1900	23.22 590	25.59 650	213 15	38 3.54	
65	Tr-1	62.9 1600	24.01 610	27.55 700	213 15	38 3.54	
66	Tr-2	52.0 1320	25.0 635	28.0 711	178 12.5	65 6.0	
67/ 68	Tk-3	50.0 1270	18.11 460	24.80 630	199 14	17 1.6	
69/ 70/71	Tv-1	55.1 1400	22.04 560	25.59 650	171 12	25 2.31	B.P. is 13Kg/cm² in some and H.S. is greater.
72	Vr-3	50.0 1270	22.44 570	25.59 650	171 12	23 2.1	
73	Pr-1	62.9 1600	22.44 570	25.59 650	171 12	23 2.1	
74	Vr-1	50.0 1270	16.92 430	21.65 550	171 12	15 1.4	
75	Vr-2	50.0 1270	17.71 450	23.62 600	171 12	16 1.5	
76	Vr-5	44.0 1118	18.0 457	24.0 609	185 13	30 2.8	

FRANCE. S.N.C.F.

1	2	3	4	5	*6	7	8
	0—4—0	48	8	24	—	—	N.S.
	L.-St.E.Ry.	1219	203	610	—	—	R. Stephenson 1828.
77	231.K.	79.1 2010	(2)17.32/(2)25.59 (2)440/(2)650	25.59 650	232 16	46 4.3	Max. A/L. 19t.
78	231.F.	76.8 1950	(2)16.53/(2)25.19 (2)420/(2)640	25.59 650	232 16	46 4.3	Max. A/L. 20t.
79	231.E.	76.8 1950	(2)16.53/(2)25.19 (2)420/(2)640	25.59 650	247 17	46 4.3	Max. A/L. 19t.
80	231.C.	75.2 1910	(2)17.32/(2)24.40 (2)440/(2)620	(2)25.98/(2)27.16 (2)660/(2)690	247 17	38 3.5	Max. A/L. 19t.
81	232.R.	78.7 2000	(3)21.26 (3)540	27.56 700	290 20	56 5.2	Stoker fired. Max. A/L. 23t.
82	232.U.	78.7 2000	(2)17.51/(2)26.77 (2)445/(2)680	27.56 700	290 20	56 5.2	Stoker fired. Max. A/L. 23t.
83	241.P.	79.1 2010	(2)17.72/(2)26.77 (2)450/(2)680	(2)25.59/(2)27.56 (2)650/(2)700	290 20	55 5.1	Stoker fired. Max. A/L. 20t.
84	241.A.	76.8 1950	(2)16.73/(2)25.98 (2)425/(2)660	28.35 720	261 18	48 4.4	Max. A/L. 20t.
85	242.A.	76.8 1950	23.62/(2)26.77 600/(2)680	23.35/(2)29.92 720/(2)760	290 20	54 5.0	Max. A/L. 21t.
86	151.A.	59.4 1510	(2)18.89/(2)29.33 (2)480/(2)745	(2)25.59/(2)27.56 (2)650/(2)700	290 20	54 5.0	Max. A/L. 19t.
87	141.C.	65 1650	24.41 620	27.56 700	203 14	41 3.8	Max. A/L. 17t.
88	141.R.	63.8 1620	23.5 597	28.0 711	225 15.5	56 5.2	Stoker or oil fired. Max. A/L. 20t.
89	141.E.	65.3 1660	(2)20.08/(2)28.35 (2)510/(2)720	(2)25.59/(2)27.56 (2)650/(2)700	232 16	46 4.3	Max. A/L. 18t.
90	141.P.	63.8 1620	(2)16.14/(2)25.19 (2)410/(2)640	27.56 700	290 20	46 4.3	Max. A/L. 19t.
91	140.C.	57.1 1450	23.22 590	25.59 650	189 13	35 3.2	B.P. 12 hpz. and 14 hpz. in others. Max. A/L. 18t.
92	150.P.	61.4 1560	(2)19.29/(2)26.77 (2)490/(2)680	(2)25.19/(2)27.56 (2)640/(2)700	261 18	38 3.5	Stoker fired. Max. A/L. 19t.
94	150.E. Est.	54.7 1390	(3)22.04 (3)560	25.98 660	203 14	36 3.3	Max. A/L. 17t.
95	230.K. P-O.	69.3 1760	19.63 500	25.59 650	174 12	30 2.8	Max. A/L. 16t.
96	230.K. Est.	81.9 2080	(2)14.57/(2)23.23 (2)370/(2)590	26.77 680	261 18	35 3.2	Grate area and H.P. cyl. diam., vary slightly in some engines.
97	230.D. Nord	69.3 1760	(2)14.96/(2)21.65 (2)380/(2)550	25.19 640	232 16	30 2.8	Max. A/L. 17t.
98	141.TA. P-O.	55.1 1400	23.62 600	25.59 650	189 13	29 2.7	B.P. 12 hpz. in some engines.
99	141.TC. Nord	61.4 1560	25.19 640	27.56 700	261 18	34 3.1	Max. A/L. 22t.

* Column 6: The boiler pressure is in lb/sq.in. and hectopiezes. 14.5 lb/sq.in. = 1 hpz.

For locomotives of German prototypes, see GERMANY (pages 168–169).

FRANCE. S.N.C.F.—*continued*

1	2	3	4	5	*6	7	8
100	141.TB. Est.	61.8 1570	21.65 550	25.98 660	203 14	26 2.4	B.P. 16 hpz. in some. Max. A/L. 16t.
101	050.TQ.	53.5 1360	20.87 630	25.98 660	174 12	30 2.8	Max. A/L. 19t.
102	151.TQ.	53.5 1360	20.87 630	25.98 660	203 14	39 3.6	Max. A/L. 18t.
103	242.TA. P.L.M.	65.3 1660	(2)16.53/(2)20.87 (2)420/(2)630	25.59 650	232 16	34 3.1	Max. A/L. 16t.

* Column 6: The boiler pressure is in lb/sq.in. and hectopiezes. 14.5 lb/sq.in. = 1 hpz.
For locomotives of German prototypes, see GERMANY (pages 168–169).

GERMAN LOCOMOTIVES OF D.B. AND OTHER RAILWAYS

1	2	3	4	5	6	7	8
	RACK AND PINION	— —	5.12 130	12.36 340	— —	— —	Probably vertical cylinders N.S.
9	2—10—0/42 O.B.B.	55.1 1400	24.80 630	25.98 660	228 16	51 4.7	
10	2—12—0/659 O.B.B.	53.1 1350	(2)20.07/(2)29.92 (2)510/(2)760	25.59 650	213 15	45 4.2	Württ. K.
33/ 118	64/S.N.C.B. Pruss. P-8	68.9 1750	22.63 575	24.80 630	171 12	28 2.6	
34	60/S.N.C.B. Pruss. S/10	77.9 1980	(4)16.92 (4)430	24.80 630	199 14	31 2.86	
44	93/S.N.C.B. Pruss. T-9/3	53.14 1350	17.71 450	24.80 630	171 12	17 1.5	
45	98/S.N.C.B. Pruss. T-16	53.14 1350	24.01 610	25.98 660	171 12	24 2.2	
46	81/S.N.C.B. Pruss. G-8/1	53.14 1350	23.62 600	25.98 660	199 14	29 2.66	Max. A/L. 17.6t.
47/ 115	25/S.N.C.B. 50	55.1 1400	23.62 600	25.98 660	228 16	42 3.9	
93	150/S.N.C.F. Pruss. G-12	55.1 1400	(3)22.44 (3)570	25.98 660	199 14	42 3.9	
104	18.608 Bav. S3/6	73.5 1870	(2)16.73/(2)25.59 (2)425/(2)650	(2)24.01/(2)26.37 (2)610/(2)670	228 16	49 4.5	
105	0-3	78.7 2000	22.44 570	25.98 660	228 16	44 4.05	
106	0-1	78.7 2000	23.62 600	25.98 660	228 16	49 4.5	
107	0-1 Reb.	78.7 2000	23.62 600	25.98 660	228 16	42 3.9	
108	0-3/10 Reb.	78.7 2000	(3)18.50 (3)470	25.98 660	228 16	41 3.8	
109	0-1/10 Reb.	78.7 2000	(3)19.68 (3)500	25.98 660	228 16	42 3.9	Oil fired.
110	10	78.7 2000	(3)18.89 (3)480	28.34 720	256 18	42 3.9	Oil fired.
112	41	62.9 1600	20.47 520	28.34 720	228 16	42 3.9	

GERMAN LOCOMOTIVES OF D.B. AND OTHER RAILWAYS—*continued*

1	2	3	4	5	6	7	8
113	41.Reb.	62.9 1600	20.47 520	28.34 720	228 16	42 3.87	
114/ 304	44 D.B. 56.T.C.D.D.	55.1 1400	(3)21.65 (3)550	25.98 660	228 16	57 4.7	
116	42/F.C.	55.1 1400	23.62 600	25.98 660	199 14	25 2.3	
117	50/Crosti	55.1 1400	23.62 600	25.98 660	228 16	33 3.05	
119	23	68.9 1750	21.65 550	25.98 660	228 16	34 3.1	
120	24	59.0 1500	19.68 500	25.98 660	199 14	22 2.05	
121	64	59.0 1500	19.68 500	25.98 660	199 14	22 2.05	
122	93 Pruss. T-14/1	53.1 1350	23.62 600	25.98 660	171 12	27 2.5	
123	74 Pruss. T-12	59.0 1500	21.25 540	24.80 630	171 12	18 1.7	
124	86	55.1 1400	22.44 570	25.98 660	199 14	37 2.4	
125	82	55.1 1400	23.62 600	25.98 660	199 14	36 2.3	
126	66	62.9 1600	18.50 470	25.98 660	228 16	21 1.9	
127	65	59.0 1500	22.44 570	25.98 660	199 14	29 2.7	
215	C.F.L. 5222 Pruss. G-10	55.1 1400	24.80 630	25.98 660	171 12	28 2.6	
218/ 312	52	55.1 1400	23.62 600	25.98 660	228 16	42 3.9	
219	C.F.L. 3023 Pruss. T-9/1	53.1 1350	16.92 430	24.80 630	171 12	16 1.5	N.S.

GREAT BRITAIN. B.R.

1	2	3	4	5	6	7	8
	Trevithick's 0—4—0	45 1143	8.25 210	54.00 1371	— —	— —	(Probably) single vertical cylinder. N.S.
128	"Schools" V	79 2006	(3)16.5 (3)420	26 660	220 15.46	28.3 2.63	
129	4—4—0 Class 2	81 2057	19 483	26 660	180 12.65	21.1 1.95	
129	4—6—2 "W.C."	74 1879	(3)16.375 (3)416	24 610	250 17.57	38.25 3.55	B.P. orig. 280 lb/sq.in.
130	2—6—0 K-3/2	68 1727	(3)18.5 (3)470	26 660	180 12.65	28 2.6	

169

1	2	3	4	5	6	7	8
131	2—6—0 B.R. 4	63 1600	17.5 445	26 660	225 15.82	23 2.13	
132	4—6—0 "Hall"	72 1828	18.5 470	30 762	225 15.82	27 2.5	
133	4—6—0 B.R. 5	74 1879	19 483	28 711	225 15.82	28.7 2.67	
134	4—6—0 "King"	78 1930	(4)16.25 (4)413	28 711	250 17.57	34.3 3.18	
135	Reb. "Royal Scot", L.M.S.	81 2057	(3)18 (3)457	26 660	250 17.57	31.25 2.89	
136	"Coronation" L.M.S.	81 2057	(4)16.5 (4)420	28 711	250 17.57	50 4.64	
137	Reb. "W.C." Southern	74 1879	(3)16.375 (3)416	24 610	250 17.57	38.25 3.55	
138	A-4 L.N.E.	80 2032	(3)18.5 (3)470	26 660	250 17.57	41.25 3.83	
139	A-1 L.N.E.	80 2032	(3)19 (3)483	26 660	250 17.57	50 4.64	
140	4—6—2 B.R. 8	74 1879	(3)18 (3)457	28 711	250 17.57	48.6 4.51	
141	4—6—2 "Britannia"	74 1879	20 508	28 711	250 17.57	42 3.9	
142	V-2 L.N.E.	74 1879	(3)18.5 (3)470	26 660	220 15.46	41.25 3.83	
143	2—8—0 28XX	55.5 1409	18.5 470	30 762	225 15.82	27 2.5	
144	O-4/3 G.C.R.	56 1422	21 534	26 660	180 12.65	26.24 2.43	
145	2—8—0 Stanier 8F	56.5 1434	18.5 470	28 711	225 15.82	28.6 2.66	
146	B.R. 9F	60 1524	20 508	28 711	250 17.57	40.2 3.73	
147	B.R. 9F Ex Crosti	60 1524	20 508	28 711	250 17.57	40.2 3.73	
148	0—6—0 Mid. 3F	63 1600	18.5 470	26 660	175 12.5	21 1.95	N.S.
149	0—6—0 Caledonian	60 1524	18.5 470	26 660	180 12.65	20 1.86	
149	4—6—0 L.M. 5	72 1828	18.5 470	28 711	225 15.82	28.6 2.66	
150	Q-1 Southern	61 1554	19 483	26 660	230 16.17	27 2.5	
151	2—6 2T G.W. 41XX	68 1727	18 457	30 762	200 14.06	20.3 2.88	
152	2—6—4T B.R. 4	68 1727	18 457	28 711	225 15.82	26.7 2.48	
153	0—6—0PT G.W.	55.5 1409	17.5 445	24 610	200 14.06	15.3 1.42	N.S.
154	L-1 L.N.E.	62 1574	20 508	26 660	225 15.82	24.7 2.29	Cyls. in some are 18.5in. diam.
155	Z Southern	56 1422	(3)16 (3)407	28 711	180 12.65	18.6 1.73	

GREECE. C.E.H.

1	2	3	4	5	6	7	8
156	0—6—0T Δα	54 1362	16.5 420	24 610	210 14.7	20 1.8	N.S.
157	2—10—2 Mα	63 1600	26 660	27.5 700	256 18	60 5.6	T.E. 56,500 lb at 75%
158	2—10—0 Λγ	57 1448	21 534	28 712	213 15	50 4.6	
159	2—10—0 Λα	55.5 1410	24.01 610	28.34 720	199 14	48 4.4	
160/ 304	2—8—0 Θγ	57 1448	19 483	26 660	225 15.8	41 3.8	
161	0—10—0 Κβ	51.1 1300	23.23 590	24.88 632	185 13	37 3.4	Austrian Süd. Type 80 design.
162	0—10—0 Κγ	51.1 1300	23.23 590	24.88 632	185 13	37 3.4	

GREECE. S.P.A.P. METRE GAUGE

1	2	3	4	5	6	7	8
163	2—8—0 E	47.2 1200	19.68 500	21.65 550	171 12	23 2.16	
164	2—6—0T Z	43.3 1100	12.99 330	19.68 500	142 10	11 1.02	N.S.
165	2—6—0T Zs	47.2 1200	16.53 420	19.68 500	156 11	13 1.17	
166	2—8—2 BredaΔ	47.2 1200	18.5 470	24.01 610	185 13	31 2.86	
167	2—8—2 Vul.Δ	48 1220	16 407	24 610	200 14	28 2.6	T.E. 21,760 lb.

HOLLAND. N.S.

1	2	3	4	5	6	7	8
	De Arend 2—2—2	72 1828	14 355	16.75 425	— —	— —	N.S.
168/ 169	PO/3	72.8 1850	(4)15.75 (4)400	25.98 660	171 12	31 2.84	
170	PO/4	72.8 1850	(4)16.53 (4)420	25.98 660	199 14	34 3.16	
171	PO/1 1718	84.6 2150	20.00 508	25.98 660	156 11	23 2.10	
172	PO/1 1912	79.4 2016	19.68 500	25.98 660	149 10.5	22 2.04	
173	PO/2	82·7 2100	20.86 530	25.98 660	176 12.4	26 2.4	

HOLLAND N.S.—*continued*

1	2	3	4	5	6	7	8
174	GO/2	59.8 1520	19.68 500	24.01 610	176 12.4	24 2.2	
175	W.D.	56.5 1435	19 483	28 712	225 15.8	28 2.66	British Austerity.
176	ZG-1 4701	53.1 1350	(3)19.68 (3)500	25.98 660	185 13	33 3.02	T.G.O.J. design.
177	4001	74.4 1890	(3)19.68 (3)500	25.98 660	171 12	35 3.25	Bergslagernas Ry. design.
178	PTO/2	79.1 2010	19.68 500	25.98 660	149 10.5	22 2.04	
179	PTO/3	72.8 1850	20.00 508	25.98 660	171 12	26 2.4	
180	PTO/4	72.8 1850	(4)16.53 (4)420	25.98 660	171 12	31 2.84	Cylinders later were 400mm diam.
181	R/2-L/3	43.3 1100	14.56 370	18.89 480	166 11.7	13 1.23	N.S.
182	RO/1	55.1 1400	19.09 485	23.62 600	171 12	16 1.47	
183	GTO/3	61 1550	(4)16.53 (4)420	25.98 660	199 14	34 3.16	

IRELAND

1	2	3	4	5	6	7	8
	Vauxhall 2—2—0	60 1524	11 280	17 432	—	—	Reb. as 2—2—2T 1840.

IRELAND. C.I.E.

1	2	3	4	5	6	7	8
184	0—6—0 J-15	61.75 1568	18 457	24 610	160 11.25	18 1.67	Z class sup. boiler. B.P. 150 in non-sup. boilers.
185	4—4—0 D-4	68.5 1739	18 457	26 660	180 12.65	20 1.86	B.P. was 160 in some engines.
186	0—6—2T L-3	66 1676	18 457	24 610	160 11.25	18 1.67	
187	4—6—0 B-la	79 2006	(3)18.5 (3)470	28 711	225 15.82	33.5 3.1	
188	2—6—0 K-1	66 1676	19 483	28 711	200 14.06	25 2.32	

IRELAND. U.T.A.

1	2	3	4	5	6	7	8
189	4—4—0 U-2	72 1828	19 483	24 610	170 11.9	21.1 1.96	T.E. 15,606 lb.
190	2—6—0 W	72 1828	19 483	26 660	200 14.06	25 2.32	T.E. 22,160 lb.
191	2—6—4T WT	72 1828	19 483	26 660	200 14.06	25 2.32	T.E. 22,160 lb.

IRELAND. G.N.R.

1	2	3	4	5	6	7	8
192	4—4—2T T-1	69 1752	18 457	24 610	175 12.5	18.3 1.7	
193	0—6—4T RT	51 1295	17 432	24 610	175 12.5	16.3 1.51	T.E. 18,074 lb. N.S.
194	0—6—0 UG	61 1854	18 457	24 610	200 14.06	18.3 1.7	T.E. 21,671 lb.
195	4—4—0 VS	79 2006	(3)15.25 (3)387	26 660	220 15.46	25.2 2.34	T.E. 21,462 lb.
196	4—4—0 U	69 1752	18 457	24 610	200 14.06	18.3 1.7	

ITALY. F.S.

1	2	3	4	5	6	7	8
	Bayard 2—2—2	67 1702	14 356	16.75 425	50 3.5	— —	N.S.
197	4—6—2 691	79.9 2030	(4)17.71 (4)450	26.77 680	228 16	46 4.3	
198	2—8—2 746	74.0 1880	(2)19.29/(2)28.34 (2)490/(2)720	26.77 680	199 14	46 4.3	
199	2—6—0 640	72.8 1850	21.25 540	27.55 700	171 12	26 2.4	
200	2—8—0 745	64.2 1630	22.83 580	28.34 720	171 12	41 3.8	
201/ 202	2—6—2 683/685	72.8 1850	(4)16.53 (4)420	25.59 650	171 12	38 3.5	
203	2—6—0 623	60.2 1530	19.29 490	27.55 700	171 12	26 2.4	
204	0—10—0 471	53.9 1370	(2)14.76/(2)24.01 (2)375/(2)610	25.59 650	228 16	38 3.5	Plancher Compound.
205	2—10—0 480	53.9 1370	26.37 670	25.59 650	171 12	49 4.3	
206/ 207	2—8—0 740/741	53.9 1370	21.25 540	27.55 700	171 12	30 2.8	
208	2—8—0 735	53.9 1370	21.25 540	27.55 700	171 12	35 3.2	
209	2—6—0T 875	59.4 1510	15.35 390	22.83 580	171 12	16 1.5	N.S.
210	0—6—0T 835	51.6 1310	16.53 420	22.83 580	171 12	16 1.5	N.S.
211	0—8—0WT 896	43.1 1095	21.25 540	20.47 520	171 12	17 1.6	

ITALY. F.N.M.

1	2	3	4	5	6	7	8
212	0—4—0T 200	56.9 1446	12.59 320	23.62 600	156 11	13 1.2	N.S.
213	4—6—0WT 280	63.8 1620	19.68 500	23.62 600	171 12	26 2.4	

LUXEMBOURG. C.F.L.

1	2	3	4	5	6	7	8
216	2—10—0	49.2	(3)22.04	23.62	199	48.4	
	P-H./0-1	1250	(3)560	600	14	4.48	
217	2—8—0	57.07	21.65	27.95	228	44	
	Liberation	1450	550	710	16	4.09	
219	2—6—2T	62.9	19.68	24.8	171	—	
	P-H./H-1	1600	500	630	12	—	
220	2—6—2T	62.9	21.25	25.19	171	—	
	P-H./L	1600	540	640	12	—	
221	2—4—2T	62.6	16.92	23.62	171	—	
	P-H./E	1590	430	600	12	—	
222	0—8—0T	49.2	19.68	24.8	171	—	
	P-H./G-1	1250	500	630	12	—	
223	0—8—0T	47.2	18.89	23.62	171	—	
	P-H./G	1200	480	600	12	—	

For locomotives of German prototypes, see GERMANY (pages 168–169).

NORWAY. N.S.B.

1	2	3	4	5	6	7	8
	2—4—0	57	15	22	100	—	R. Stephenson.
	N.H.J. 1851	1447	381	558	7	—	N.S.
224/	2—8—4	60.2	(2)17.32/(2)25.59	(2)25.59/(2)27.55	248	54	T.E. 45,000 lb.
225	49C	1530	(2)440/(2)650	(2)650/(2)700	17	5.0	
226	4—6—0	62.9	17.71	23.62	171	—	
	27	1600	450	600	12	—	
227	4—6—0	62.9	(4)14.96	23.62	185	26	
	30a	1600	(4)390	600	13	2.4	
228	4—8—0	53.1	(2)14.96/(2)23.03	23.62	220	—	
	26c	1350	(2)390/(2)585	600	15.5	—	
229	4—8—0	53.1	(2)16.53/(2)24.80	23.62	228	33	
	31b	1350	(2)420/(2)630	600	16	3.0	
230	2—10—0	49.2	25.59	25.19	171	36	
	39	1250	650	640	12	3.32	
231	2—8—0	49.2	22.63	25.19	171	—	
	33a	1250	575	640	12	—	
232	2—6—0	56.8	16.73/25.00	24.01	171	—	
	21a	1445	425/635	610	12	—	N.S.
233	2—6—0	56.8	17.00	24.01	171	—	
	21b	1445	432	610	12	—	
234	0—6—0T	41.7	14.17	19.68	171	—	
	25d	1060	360	500	12	—	
235	2—8—2T	53.1	22.04	23.62	171	—	
	34a	1350	560	600	12	—	
236	2—6—2T	62.9	20.66	23.62	171	—	
	32c	1600	525	600	12	—	

PORTUGAL. C.P. BROAD GAUGE

1	2	3	4	5	6	7	8
237	4—6—0 270	68.9 1750	(2)13.77/(2)21.65 (2)350/(2)550	25.19 640	213 15	31 2.91	N.S.
238	4—6—0 355	74.8 1900	(2)14.96/(2)22.83 (2)380/(2)580	25.19 640	228 16	34 3.18	
239	4—6—0 235	60.6 1545	(2)13.77/(2)21.65 (2)350/(2)550	25.59 650	199 14	31 2.88	
240	4—6—2 553	74.8 1900	(2)14.96/(2)22.83 (2)380/(2)580	25.19 640	228 16	41 3.84	
241	4—6—2 502	74.8 1900	(2)14.96/(2)22.83 (2)380/(2)580	25.19 640	228 16	41 3.82	
242	2—8—0 763	51.2 1300	(2)14.17/(2)23.22 (2)360/(2)590	25.59 650	228 16	38 3.52	N.S.
243	2—8—0 707	52.4 1330	22.04 560	24.80 630	171 12	31 2.84	T.E. 29,400 lb at 75%.
244	4—8—0 803	64.2 1630	(2)16.53/(2)25.19 (2)420/(2)640	25.59 650	228 16	43 3.97	T.E. 28,880 lb at 50%.
245	2—8—2 872	60 1524	21 533	28 711	199 14	47 4.36	T.E. 35,000 lb.
246	0—6—0 23	51 1295	18 457	24 610	114 8	17 1.54	N.S.
247	4—8—0 834	63 1600	24.40 620	25.98 660	199 14	49 4.56	
248	2—6—2T 039	55.5 1409	19.01 483	24.40 620	185 13	26 2.42	N.S.
249	2—6—2T 041	60.8 1546	18.11 460	23.62 600	171 12	26 2.44	N.S.
250	0—6—2T 011	48 1220	19.01 483	25.98 660	142 10	20 1.89	N.S.
251	2—8—4T 0224	53.1 1350	24.01 610	25.98 660	185 13	39 3.6	
252	2—6—4T 071	59.8 1520	20.47 520	25.19 640	171 12	27 2.53	

PORTUGAL. C.P. METRE GAUGE

1	2	3	4	5	6	7	8
253	2—6—0T E.84	39.4 1000	13.78 350	19.68 500	142 10	12 1.09	ex Companhia Nacional, 1887.
254	2—8—2T E.141	53.1 1350	17.71 450	23.62 600	171 12	21 1.9	T.E. 21,936 lb at 75%
255	4—6—0T E.124	43.3 1100	14.17 360	21.65 550	171 12	14 1.3	
256	Mallet T E.165	43.3 1100	(2)12.59/(2)18.89 (2)320/(2)480	21.65 550	171 12	15 1.37	
357	Mallet T E.181	43.3 1100	(2)13.77/(2)19.68 (2)350/(2)500	21.65 550	199 14	22 2.0	T.E. 19,030 lb at 75%.

1	2	3	4	5	6	7	8
	MATARO	72.0 1828	13.8 350	19.7 500	85 6	— —	N.S.
259	030.2077	59.0 1500	17.32 440	23.62 600	128 9	23 2.1	N.S.
260	040.2514	51.2 1300	21.65 550	25.59 650	171 12	23 2.1	
261	230.2096	68.8 1750	21.65 550	25.59 650	171 12	28 2.6	
262	230.4051	68.8 1750	(2)13.77/(2)21.65 (2)350/(2)550	25.59 650	199 14	29 2.7	N.S. Slide valves.
262	240.4069	63.0 1600	(2)16.53/(2)25.19 (2)420/(2)640	25.59 650	228 16	44 4.1	
263	130.2114	59.0 1500	21.25 540	24.01 610	171 12	40 3.7	
264	231.4021	66.1 1680	(2)15.74/(2)24.40 (2)400/(2)620	25.59 650	228 16	44 4.1	
265	140.2263	61.4 1560	24.01 610	25.59 650	171 12	33 3.0	
266	140.2438	61.4 1560	24.01 610	25.59 650	185 13	33 3.0	
267	141.2007	61.4 1560	23.00 584	25.23 641	180 12.7	44 4.1	
268	141F.2397	61.4 1560	22.44 570	27.95 710	213 15	52 4.8	
269	240.2213	63.0 1600	24.40 620	25.98 660	199 14	49 4.5	
270	240F.2629	64.2 1630	24.01 610	27.95 710	242 17	56 5.2	T.E. 39,402 lb. Max. A/L. 19.5t.
271/ 272	241.4020	68.8 1750	(2)18.11/(2)27.55 (2)460/(2)700	26.77 680	228 16	54 5.0	
273	241.2103	68.8 1750	22.04 560	27.95 710	256 18	54 5.0	B.P. orig. 20 Kg/cm.²
274	241.2078	68.8 1750	24.40 620	27.95 710	199 14	53 4.9	
275	241F.2210	68.8 1750	25.19 640	27.95 710	228 16	57 5.3	
276	242F.2008	74.8 1900	25.19 640	27.95 710	228 16	57 5.3	
277	060.4004	47.2 1200	(2)15.74/(2)23.62 (2)400/(2)600	23.62 600	185 13	26 2.4	
278	151.3115	61.4 1560	(3)22.44 (3)570	29.52 750	228 16	57 5.3	
279	462F.0404	68.8 1750	(4)19.05 (4)484	25.98 660	199 14	53 4.9	
280	282F.0424	47.2 1200	(4)17.32 (4)440	24.01 610	213 15	46 4.3	
281	040.0231	47.9 1220	20.47 520	25.59 650	171 12	24 2.2	N.S.
282	242.0406	61.4 1560	(2)15.74/(2)24.40 (2)400/(2)620	25.19 640	228 16	34 3.1	
282	242.0255	63.0 1600	23.62 600	25.98 660	171 12	44 4.1	

SWEDEN. S.J.

1	2	3	4	5	6	7	8
	FORSTLINGEN 0—4—0	25.2 640	8.26 210	15.74 400	50 3.5	— —	N.S.
284	4—6—0 B	68.9 1750	23.22 590	24.40 620	171 12	28 2.6	
285	4—6—0 A-6	67.4 1712	20.47 520	24.01 610	171 12	26 2.4	
286	0—8—0 E	54.6 1388	19.68 500	25.19 640	171 12	22 2.1	
287	0—8—0 E-4	50.2 1275	21.65 550	25.19 640	142 10	23 2.2	
288	2—8—0 E-2	54.6 1388	19.68 500	25.19 640	171 12	22 2.1	
289	4—6—0 A-3	67.3 1710	20.47 520	24.01 610	171 12	28 2.6	
290	0—10—0 R	51.2 1300	27.55 700	25.19 640	171 12	34 3.1	
291	4—8—0 E-10	55.1 1400	(3)17.71 (3)450	24.01 610	199 14	28 2.6	
292	2—6—4T S-1	55.1 1400	18.50 470	24.01 610	185 13	20 1.8	
293	0—8—0T N	47.6 1210	18.89 480	23.62 600	171 12	19 1.7	
294	2—6—2T S-7	55.1 1400	18.50 470	24.01 610	156 11	20 1.8	
295	2—6—4T J	51.2 1300	16.53 420	22.83 580	171 12	15 1.4	

SWITZERLAND. S.B.B.

1	2	3	4	5	6	7	8
	LIMMAT 4—2—0	60.2 1530	14.17 360	22.04 560	85 6	9 0.87	N.S.
296	4—6—0 A3/5	70.0 1780	(2)14.17/(2)22.44 (2)360/(2)570	25.98 660	213 15	28 2.6	N.S.
297	2—10—0 C5/6	52.4 1330	(2)18.50/(2)27.16 (2)470/(2)690	25.19 640	213 15	40 3.7	
298	2—6—2T Eb 3/5	60.6 1540	21.25 540	23.62 600	171 12	26 2.4	
299	0—8—0T E4/4	52.4 1330	20.47 520	25.19 640	171 12	19 1.7	
300	0—6—0WT E3/3	40.9 1040	14.17 360	19.68 500	171 12	12.5 1.2	N.S.
301	2—6—0T Ec 3/4	52.4 1330	16.23 420	25.59 650	171 12	19 1.7	N.S.
302	2—6—2T Eb 3/5	59.8 1520	20.47 520	23.62 600	171 12	25 2.3	

TURKEY. T.C.D.D.

1	2	3	4	5	6	7	8
	OTTOMAN RY. Nos. 1-10	61 1550	16 406	22 559	135 9.49	12 1.11	N.S.
303	2—8—2	68.9 1750	25.59 650	25.98 660	228 16	43 4.00	T.E. 47,685 lb.
305	2—10—0 Skoda	57.1 1450	25.59 650	25.98 660	228 16	45 4.2	T.E. 57,560 lb.
306	2—10—0 Vulcan U.S.	57.1 1450	23.50 597	28 711	250 17.6	58 5.37	T.E. 58,300 lb. Stoker fired.
307	4—8—0	65 1650	24.80 630	25.98 660	171 12	33 3.03	T.E. 35,840 lb.
308	2—8—0 G-8/2	55.1 1400	24.80 630	25.98 660	199 14	37 3.4	T.E. 48,930 lb.
309	2—8—2 R.S.	62 1575	19.50 495	26 660	170 11.95	25 2.35	
310	2—8—2 Baldwin	60 1524	21 534	28 711	203 14	47 4.37	T.E. 35,000 lb.
311	2—10—0 C. Louvert	53.1 1350	24.80 630	24.01 610	185 13	39 3.65	T.E. 43,633 lb.
313	2—6—0 (2—4—2—2)	59 1500	21.25 540	24.80 630	171 12	24 2.25	
314	2—8—0	57.1 1450	21.65 550	25.98 660	171 12	28 2.6	
315	2—10—2	55.1 1400	24.80 630	25.98 660	171 12	33 3.03	T.E. 41,760 lb.
316	2—10—2T 3-cyl.	55.1 1400	(3)22.44 (3)570	31.18 792	228 16	43 4.0	T.E. 68,847 lb.
317	2—6—2T	55.5 1410	19.68 500	24.80 630	171 12	30 2.75	
318	4—6—4T T-18	65 1650	22.04 560	24.80 630	171 12	26 2.44	
319	0—4—0ST	48.5 1231	15 381	22 559	135 9.49	10 0.97	N.S.
320	0—6—0T	49.2 1250	16.92 430	24.80 630	171 12	16 1.5	N.S.
321	0—8—2T	54.5 1384	19.50 495	26 660	180 12.65	25 2.35	N.S.

ACKNOWLEDGEMENTS

In the preparation of this book I have had access to the official locomotive records of most of the railways concerned. Wherever possible these have been checked by reference to at least one other source of information and this has been achieved only by consulting many books and builders' catalogues. *The Locomotive* has, as always, provided a mass of useful information and the relevant sections of *The Concise Encyclopaedia of World Railway Locomotives* have also been of great value.

My thanks are due to the railway administrations of the countries mentioned, all of whom have given me many privileges and who, with one exception, have replied promptly and fully to my several enquiries. To Othmar Bamer in Austria, Maurice Maillet in France, Gustavo Reder in Spain, Erik Sundstrom in Sweden and to P. M. Kalla Bishop I owe a great debt, not only for reading and checking proofs, but also for supplying me with information which was seemingly unobtainable elsewhere. Most of all I owe to my greatly respected friend, the late Hugh le Fleming, from whom I learned so much of European locomotives and their designers.